SOUL and SPIRIT PSYCHOLOGY
REVISED EDITION

By Aquarian

Published by

halfabook.com

Soul and Spirit Psychology
Second Edition January, 2023

The views and opinions contained in this book are not those of the publisher. This
book was published in the spirit of free thought, that people may continue to think,
grow, discuss ideas, and share the deep thoughts that form our inner beliefs. We
encourage you to exercise free will, accept whatever truth you choose to believe,
but above all, think and understand.

Manufactured in the United States of America

Soul and Spirit Psychology
version 2 January, 2023
Philosophy
Metaphysics

ISBN   978-1-58884-036-3   (print)
           978-1-58884-037-0   (eBook)

Table of Contents

....2
INTRODUCTION...5
MEDITATION...11
  1. THE SPIRITUAL PATH..13
  2. WHAT ISN'T MEDITATION...26
  3. MEDITATION IS...28
  4. DANGERS OF MEDITATION 35
  5. LONG MEDITATIONS..40
  6. BEST TIME TO MEDITATE...44
  7. RELAXATION...47
  8. POSTURES...51
  9. MANTRAS..57
GOD, SPIRIT, & SOUL 63
  10. GOD CHARACTERISTICS..65
  11. SOUL CHARACTERISTICTICS 77
  12. THE OUTER SELF...107
  12. THE OUTER SELF...107
  13. ELIMINATING ADDICTIONS...126
  14. SEX...131
  15. WEALTH 140
  16. BREATH FOLLOWING...143
MIND...147
  17. MASS MIND..149
  18. COMMON SENSE..151
  19. EMOTIONAL MIND...152
  20. INTELLECTUAL MIND..154
  21. CONTEMPLATIVE MIND..160
  22. INTUITIVE MIND...163
  23. PSYCHIC KNOWLEDGE...167
  24. CONTEMPLATION PRACTICES..170
  25. THOUGHT CONTROL...172
  26. TIPS FOR SEEKERS 192
  27. RIGHT LIVELIHOOD...198
  28. HEALING...205
  29. DIET...213
  30. FINALLY...219

INTRODUCTION

I am Aquarian. My spiritual path started with Christianity at the age of 23. I attended five different protestant churches, became a member of three. I read the Holy Bible once, and the new testament four times. The Bible left me with many questions that no one knew how to answer. So that part of the path dead ended for me. However a couple of years later, a new path opened up.

Something struck me ---- I stood up one evening, drove to a library and walked down the main aisle. Turned left at another aisle, walked 10 feet, turned left again, and focused on a book. I was spiritually led to the book, but didn't know it. I knew what I was doing, yet did not know what I was doing. That's what being led and informed by God feels like.

The book was interesting, but it didn't add any knowledge about higher spirituality. However the Rosicrucians were twice mentioned, so I searched for their address and sent them a letter about joining their organization. This is a 3000 year old religion that came from ancient Egypt. A lot of good lessons were taught about higher spirituality, and some new lessons on being psychic. Unfortunately, I had to stop the lessons due to becoming extremely sensitive.

A year later, the path was picked up again when surrendering to God. Once again I knew when and where to go, and that I needed to be there on June 16. So I arrived on Maui, Hawaii on the 16th. I spoke with a local person who said that there was a commune on the island's north side. I hitched a ride and amazingly, about 1/2 mile from the commune was a Zendo, which is a Zen Meditation Center.

I got out and talked with a teacher. His Zendo was full, but he had a halfway house a quarter mile away. They did Hatha yoga, but that is a muscle religion. Nothing was being learned there of value that was spiritual. Six months later, I was able to join the Zendo. Three months after studying and meditating there I became enlightened.

After that I landed back in California. Then came the problem of how to relate with others when centered in the soul. I was in this world, but not of it. Everyone around me was acting like a 10 year old child, or they were half crazy. It seemed to be a tough life to live, but it was easy, because God was with me, leading and informing. I wandered for years. A problem soul centered people have is their spotlight of attention has to remain focused on the soul. Having a job is distracting in that attention has to be turned outward for eight hours a day.

The solution was to camp all by myself during two week vacations, at a beautiful lake. The time was spent reading Alice Bailey books. This would center me back in the soul, but the high would only last six months. So the next solution was to "know thyself". That means lots of self study and contemplation. Self awareness is the answer. Self awareness has to be combined with daily meditation. Meditate after awakening, and before going to bed. That's how to grow more spiritual.

It took twenty years for me to write this book and countless meditations on the subjects. The oiginal title of the book was meditation and spiritual psychology, but I realized there was more to it than that. It should be spirit and soul psychology.

The front cover shows your inner and outer selfs. The three balls of light are God's energy. These lights enter a baby's body on the first breath, and exit the body at death. Therefore God is life. God is inside of you. Therefore you are a god. The reason why you don't act like a god is because feelings and attentions are focused on the crotch, belly, chest, ego, and imagination. That's where fun and pleasures are produced.

There are two stripes shown on the front side. They illustrate genital thinking and desires. The belly strike indicates desire and food fun. Emotions and pride are produced under the chest. The ego is produced under the strike crossing your mouth and forehead's imagination spot. The two stripes are your childish nature.

Everyone thinks that their child is natural, but the stripes are only 1 inch deep. The rest of your body is composed of soul and god's energy. So if you want to get spiritual, then get rid of the childish obsession for fun, pleasure, and happiness. Getting rid of the playful child sounds depressing, and it is but it's a a mild depression like a burnout. The first step the seeker needs to make is to get rid of all addictions, and that can take years. If you're interested in seeing what the soul is like, then try fasting. Water only for three days. The morning of the fourth day is especially good. Your questions, if any, will be quickly answered. Then if you wish, start eating. One thing to notice is that your brain becomes clear from not eating. That is a step towards higher spirituality.

The second step to higher spirituality is self

awareness. A lot of self study is needed to control your emotions, pride, and out of control mind. Start off by studying the four suffering emotions of anger, fear, sadness, and shame. There's more on that in the books third section. Also do a study on pride's superiority, greatness, and heroic Glory. Those feelings also exist on the chest and close to emotions.

The last step is to study the talking ego, and imagination. There is more on this self awareness studying in the book's third section. This step to higher spirituality is to meditate daily. What works best is to meditate right after awakening, and before bedtime. Forty minutes a session works good. I prefer breath following meditation, but I am not you. So study all the practices to find what works best for you.

This book is dedicated to all the seekers, adepts, scientists, and researchers interested in spiritual psychology and the study of the soul. May you extend what it took me a lifetime to learn, that the path of mankind may be illuminated, as we all strive to attain heaven on Earth.

Aquarian

November 2022

MEDITATION

1. THE SPIRITUAL PATH

The front cover is the first thing to be explained. Human consciousness is illustrated as orange and red stripes going from the crotch to the top of the head. The stripes are only about an inch deep. Spirit is illustrated as 3 balls of light on a string of light. The white ball in the center of the head is God's Mind (intuition). The white ball in the center of the chest is God's Love, and the ball at the tip of the spine is God's Will to Good. The soul wasn't illustrated, because it is created from Spirit's radiance.

It's necessary to begin by saying, - **don't believe anything I say**. That is said to most monks that enter a Zendo. Everything in this book is to be treated as theoretical, or as a possibility. So study the book with a scientific mind. Discard anything that doesn't fit your truth, or tuck it away for further study. Insist on finding the truth, and no blind following. The highest levels of spirituality can only be reached by those seeking the truth.

I studied religion for many years, and now have my own religion, or my own -ism. I used to think that I was a Christian. Then thought that I was a Buddhist. Now I'm down to being only religion. Seekers are also developing their own -ism, like Johnism or Maryism, for it is natural to go from being a follower of a religion to being "a temple of God".

A seeker's first concern is to find a good meditation. Unfortunately, some gurus teach dead end practices, like focusing on a flower until you become a flower. The problem with that practice is, attention is being focused on something outer. In order to become the soul, attention has to **detach** from everything outer. Fortunately, there are only 3 types of meditation that are ever needed. Those are mantras, breath following, and contemplation. This book teaches the safer ones that have been used for two thousand years.

PROBATIONERS

Probationers are beginning to love Life Itself more than pleasure and treasure.

A newcomer to God's School is called a probationer. His worthiness needs to be proved by eliminating pleasures and addictions. He's therefore on probation. Probationers are able to feel God's Love radiating within their chest, and with that wondrous feeling comes a knowing that their addiction to alcohol, drugs, and promiscuous sex has to be eliminated.

The subject of religion gets to be very bewildering, due to the multitude of beliefs and practices put forth by many religions. Your whole lifetime could be spent studying Holy Books, but book learning alone is a dead end. You need to do the practices. That brings up the problem of gullibility, because some practices create a pleasurable high. Probationers then become enthralled by the high, and are convinced that this religion, or that teacher, is the only way to go. That can dead end a seeker's journey. It's best to study and join different religions, but stay loose. Be ready to change when the time feels right.

Lots of probationers join an evangelist religion. It's where their Heart's Love can be fanned into a greater brilliance by singing hymns of praise, adoration, and gratitude to God. Evangelism has existed for thousands of years, such as the Bible tells of "Sadducees who would wear sackcloth, and cover their heads with ashes. They were also willing to circle the Sea (Sea of Galilee) for one convert". Evangelism seems to be a little strange, but it's a necessary class in God's School, and shouldn't be criticized. Those that were worshipers, during a past lifetime, will usually become worshipers again in this lifetime. However, some become disenchanted with worshiping, and then move on to mysticism.

MYSTICS

Discarding pride and emotions to become the soul's peaceful Love.

Mystics are interested in spiritual feelings, such as those created by chanting, mantras, singing, visualizations, psychism, dance, crystals, psychedelic drugs, and sex magic. Psychedelic drugs are often helpful at this stage, because it temporarily dissolves the intellectual walls. Then mystics get a wider view on life. After that, many will "tune in and drop out". That's good, but after the old lifestyle has been dismissed, then psychedelics become a negative. One problem is that the inner child becomes very playful. Another problem happens when seekers conclude that psychedelics create their highest spiritual experiences, and they will want to keep it going.

That leads to a pleasurable dead end. Mystics need to move on to the next higher feeling, which is the soul's peacefulness. Meditation works well for that, because a deep peacefulness is experienced during meditation.

There are advantages to becoming a mystic, such as Love creates a social intelligence which knows the right thing to say and do. It's called wisdom, or loving understanding. Love also knows what's in the Hearts of others, because all Hearts are connected to the Heart of God. A peak mystical experience is reached when a seeker realizes that Love is their true self, or real self. No matter how highly spiritual a seeker becomes, he'll always know that Love is his real self. This is the second step of initiation, as it is very important to get a glimpse your true self.

CONTEMPLATORS

Discarding the playful outer mind to become the intuitive Mind.

The spiritual path takes a long time to travel, because most are convinced that religion is all about feelings. That's true for many, because that's where their lessons are at. However, when seekers learn how to **detach** from their emotions, and become centered in their peaceful Heart, then the next lesson is learning how to shut down their fun loving brain. Meditation is **absolutely** necessary for doing that. You need to **see** what the outer mind is doing, in order to control its' playfulness.

The soul thinks in a questioning manner, so it's important to become inquisitive. Having a job that requires lots of searching, examining, defining, or trouble shooting is helpful, because attention remains in questioning mood for longer periods of time.

Pondering on a question makes the senses, desires, and emotions disappear. The best questions to contemplate on are the nearly impossible ones, like the Zen koan of "What is MU?" Everyone starts out by searching through the memory banks for information on MU, but there are no memories about MU. The alternative is to engage the intellect, and imagine some possible answers. But the intellect is like a computer. There can't be any output when there is no input. So imagining possible answers also fails. What's left is to focus on the third eye so as to perceive an answer. Then deeply ponder on the question. That moves consciousness inside the third eye tunnel to a point that's halfway between the third eye and intuition. Eventually, the intellect will slow way down, and start **looking** for an answer to appear. That's when a picture may suddenly appear from out of the ethers. God answered the question, but finding an answer is not the objective. The goal is to make the brain sit perfectly still. That's when you become the pure Mind of God.

Seekers on this level are aware that they have soul energy, and know that they can perform magic, like healing others. Jesus was a magician. He healed the sick, and walked on water. He raised the dead, and changed water into wine. That's magic. Please note that there is black magic, and there is white magic. Using your divine powers for personal gain is black magic. Such as, soul power can also be used to win a lottery. That's black. Soul power can also be used to control others. That's very black. Doing a spiritual healing, and then asking for money is black. The proper attitude is to be the hand of God that freely helps, and expects nothing in return. Receiving a donation is ok, but don't expect it.

Meditating every morning works well for creating a clear mind and healthy body. When the childish desires, emotions, and imaginings have nearly disappeared, then a contemplator needs to do a long meditation. The purpose of meditating 10 hours a day, for 7 days, is to transform from human to soul. The magical moment is called enlightenment. Three masters are present at the transformation ceremony.

ENLIGHTENMENT

Enlightenment is when a seeker becomes a Son of God. He still looks the same, but his new self is now radiating lots of God's Love, Mind, and Goodness. The reason for being called a Son of God is that he's like a young God. This is an in between consciousness that's mostly Spirit, but consciousness is still connected to the outer World.

A long meditation is needed to move up to this level. According to the ascended master Djwhal Khul, *"Enlightenment occurs when a master checks on his disciple's aura, and sees that it's of a certain size and brightness. He then contacts the Hierophant. Together, and with another master on the left side, the Hierophant will touch the top of the disciple's head with his staff. Then the body fills with light, and enlightenment happens"*. The above statement was paraphrased for clarity.

Perfect health occurs at enlightenment, due to the massive influx of Light from the masters. That makes the body rearrange itself into perfect health.

Enlightenment is known as the sudden awakening. The experience is like watching a movie at a theater. When the movie ends, and the lights of the theater are turned on, then suddenly there are people all around.

The awakening is shocking, in that another World is seen. Everything is alive. The flowers are happy and smiling. The trees are alive. Even the rocks are alive, although rocks have a fuzzy, sleepy look. Everything is composed of the One Substance called Life. That's when the Oneness of All becomes known. Heaven has always existed on Earth, but it's not known until seeing Life within everything.

Self realization also occurs at enlightenment. That happens when an enlightened person sees a ball of light within his chest. He instantly knows that this ball of light will continue to glow forever. It's also apparent that the ball of light is the real self. What this means is that **everyone** is a divine being. But they'll never know it until enlightenment happens.

Freedom is noticed when becoming a pure being. The intellectual walls have disappeared, and the soul is now freed from the imagined self. The soul is liberated, yet there is no freedom. God's energy created all of the living beings on Earth, and God is ultimately responsible for it. That's when a deep sense of responsibility towards all life happens. And that's when a Son knows that he must help to free his younger brothers from the Great Illusion.

Seeing Life within everything is astounding. What's also astounding is when seeing that everyone is engrossed in their little world of desires, emotions, and imaginings. Life now looks like something out of a science fiction novel where the World is a huge insane asylum, and everyone is walking around in a dream. Then it suddenly becomes very lonely at the top of the mountain. Now the choices are:

1. Continue living in the monastery

2. Go to the city, and be the helping hand of God.

3. Live in a cave. A newly enlightened one may wish to get away from it all when seeing that everyone is immersed in an imagined world.

Number 2 is the best choice, because the city offers lots of opportunities to make mistakes. That's important, because even the enlightened ones have more lessons to learn. Ahead will be some tough tests of whether to retry those old pleasures. Some will do it, but failure is good. The Son will know that he made a mistake, and then know the proper way to live. Years later, everything said, thought, and done will be originating from his Spirit. That's when a Son of God is on the doorstep to becoming a Man of God (adept).

ADEPTS

When all of the soul lessons have been learned, then consciousness changes from soul to Spirit, which is a Man of God. Some adepts perform astounding miracles, like the ones Jesus did. That's because they are trustworthy enough to be given the full power of God's energy.

Becoming an adept is the end of evolution on

Earth. No more incarnations are needed. However, the learning doesn't stop there. The process of evolution continues on and on in the Spirit World. Becoming a master is the next higher initiation. The ascended master Djwhal Khul (DK) claimed that "There are 4 levels of masters. After that, the masters become Planets. Then more learning ensues as the Planets have 5 spiritual levels". That statement was paraphrased for clarity. Other authors claim that planets become Suns. But evolution may not stop there, because it's logical to assume that Suns become Galaxies, and Galaxies become Cosmoses.

The wildest statement made by the master DK was that, "Someone wondered what was beyond the edge of our Cosmos. So he traveled way out and returned saying that there are other Cosmoses out there. Some are bigger. Some are smaller, and they're all connected together like on an umbilical chord". So the question becomes,- where is the outer edge of Life?. Our Cosmos has an outer edge to it, but if more Cosmoses are out there, then where does Life end?

We're now living in the Age of Aquarius. This is the Age of Enlightenment, and soul consciousness. The year 4,000 is when the Age of Capricorn starts, which is the Age of Spirit and adept consciousness. Not much can be said about the Spirit World, because Aquarians tend to be extremists. If lots of knowledge about Spirit were given, then shortcuts would be seen. Valuable lessons would be bypassed, and many would miss out on enlightenment.

This is as far as I care to go. Three nights in a row I had a strange experience during the 8:00 PM meditation. I went to the Zen teacher, he became excited and said that I was entering into the universal mind, which is the mind of planets, moons, sun, and masters. There is a barrier between the mind and universal intuition that cannot be crossed by humans, and needless to say, I couldn't get past that barrier. Neither will the experience be explained because men can use ti to make money and the insane will use it to attract followers. So there are no masters walking around earth. Edgar Cayce said that there are no masters on earth, and DK said that Jesus and the Buddha were adepts. DK said that masters can put on the physical body, but can only do it for short time because the experience is very painful.

2. WHAT ISN'T MEDITATION

Everyone has a concept of what is meditation, but they are usually wrong. It will be easier to understand what is meditation, by first examining what it isn't.

Meditation isn't:

1. Not a dream state. Consciousness exists in the here and now during meditation. That changes to the eternal now when centered in the soul.

2. Not spacing out. The spotlight disappears when a meditator becomes centered in his soul. He may look absent minded, but his consciousness is still awake and aware.

Focusing is key to meditating, and it's done by focusing attention on a spiritual practice. The insane and retarded are unable to meditate, because they are unable to remain focused.

3. Not self hypnosis. That's when the outer self becomes the master, and the inner self obeys. Meditation is the opposite. That's when the soul becomes the master, and the outer obeys.

4. Not psychism.

5. Not a trance.

6. Not staring at a Mandela, or a candle flame, because those are outer things. Those practices are also self hypnotic.

7. Not sleeping. It may look that way, but a meditator remains awake and aware. Meditation is when a person detaches from his ego and imagination. Then only bare attention is being paid to anything out there.

3. MEDITATION IS

The reason for meditating is to connect with the peaceful Heart and still Mind of your Spirit.

The spiritual Heart's radiant energy interacts with the chest to produce feelings and emotions, while the spiritual Mind's radiant light interacts with brain cells to produce thoughts. Meditators are learning how to make the outer self's emotions, imaginings, and thoughts disappear. Then they're able to go deeper within to touch their divine Heart and Mind. What this means is that mankind's spiritual nature is another branch of Psychology. It could be called Basic Psychology, or Spiritual Psychology.

Everyone becomes trapped in a World of feelings and imaginings, during early childhood. Unfortunately, most will remain focused on their outer self's feelings and imaginings during their entire life, and will only go within during times of guilt, sadness, and worry. However, some will prefer to go within by attending church and praying. Others will prefer to go way deep within by meditating. That's when a **total escape** from the outer self, and outer World happens, and that's when a different reality is experienced. One that's more real than the outer self's feelings, imaginings, and desires.

The technique of meditation is to ignore everything outer. Then attention turns inward, and connects with the Spirit's Heart and Mind. The first task of meditation is to sit perfectly still. That makes the body disappear. The second task is to relax. That makes the emotions and desires disappear. Consciousness then moves inward to the Heart's deep peacefulness. The final task is to make the mind sit perfectly still. Meditation is absolutely necessary for learning how to do that trick. When attention stops focusing on the forehead's frontal cortex, then the brain stops creating mental pictures. Remain detached from the frontal cortex, and consciousness will slowly move rearward to enter the intuitive Mind. That's when a meditator becomes the detached observer. The outer World is still being seen, but only bare attention is being paid to anything outer.

Our minds were like a radiant ball of light during early childhood. Then around the age of 2, we started to mentally focus forward. That created an attention spotlight, and we could more easily recall things. The age of 10 is when we learned how to create possibilities. Unfortunately, most will never go beyond the intellect to enter the intuitive Mind. Their entire life will be spent using the spotlight for thinking. That changes when learning how to meditate. When the spotlight stops focusing outward, then the head becomes like a radiant ball of light again. So it could be said that we meditate to become like a little child again.

Meditation is like reading a book, and being oblivious to anything around. The focus doesn't have to be intense to make the World go away. You only have to stop paying attention to the senses, body, desires, pride, emotions, imaginings, internal talker, and, memories. Then life feels peaceful, natural, and easy.

Seekers remain awake and aware during meditation. The eyes are seeing, but are only gazing at a spot on the floor about 3 feet away (a meter). Sounds are heard, but ignored. The meditator has to sit perfectly still, because **not** moving a muscle makes the body disappear. The next thing to do is relax the emotions. The relaxation practices, in chapter 7, work well for detaching from the emotions. The HUM, UM, or MM mantras also help to relax the emotions, and turn attention inward. After that, do a breath following practice to experience the ultimate in deep peacefulness. When the breath becomes ultra slow, then the peaceful soul is entered.

Another meditation practice is to deeply contemplate. Start out by having a question, and then focus on the 3rd eye to perceive an answer. That makes everything outer disappear. Next, ponder deeply on the question. That makes consciousness go inside the 3rd eye tunnel to a place that's halfway to the intuition. Eventually, the intellect will slow way down to where it's only **watching and waiting** for an answer to appear. When the outer mind is finally still, then you become the detached observer, which is soul consciousness.

The above explains how meditation works, but **why** would anyone want to meditate? Scientific studies have shown that better physical, emotional, and mental health is gained. That's nice, but the best reason is that your soul has been calling since the age of 21. Childish fun has mostly disappeared by the age of 30, and the soul is then calling a lot louder. And the call gets louder with each passing decade. So at some point, you should think about learning how to go within, and become the soul.

Meditation has two purposes. Some want to become the peaceful soul, while others wish to keep their minds steady and focused. Both paths lead to being centered in the spirit of god, which is the three white balls of light, illustrated on the front cover. Another way of explaining meditation is to say that consciousness is moving from intellect to intuition. Emotional feelings and internal talking is being made silent by relaxing the front side's desires, pride, and emotions by relaxing and focusing on the soothing outgoing breath (breath following practices). Those practices center consciousness in the peaceful, which is half nervous system and half light of spirit. The other way to become intuitive is first relax, and become a peaceful soul, then hold the imagination and intellect steady by focusing on a question. That moves consciousness to the center of the head were intuition resides. So in summary the mind is held still by becoming ultra peaceful. The other practice holds the mind steady by focusing on a question. The advantage of making the mind sit still by being deeply peaceful is better health. And the advantage of holding the mind steady by remaining focused on a question is a lot more can get done during the day. It might be better to dismiss thoughts and let them go.

I attended a sesshin, a week long meditation lasting ten hours a day. Twenty two seekers attended the sesshin. Two of them dropped out. Nobody knew why they quit. Six became enlightened. The teacher said that was an unusually high number, that usually about two become enlightened per sesshin. It was fairly easy to see which ones made it, for they stood like statues. They had no desire to move a muscle. Some women put on a cookies and milk party that evening, but I didn't attend, because nobody told me. Plus I knew in my chest not to waste time on a party. Later i attended the 30 day Buddhist type of meditation, a Dahtan held high in the Colorado mountains. So many of us attended this long meditation and it was a lot different than the Zen sesshin. We were allowed to talk and three of the seventy dropped out. One was a woman that was highly sexual. Another was a man that smoked marijuana every day. The third bunked in an A frame house with me. After the last meditation at 8:00 PM, he would start drinking from a bottle of gin. He lasted 12 days. The smoker lasted 10 days, and the woman lasted 6 days. Obviously long meditations and pleasures are not compatible. Its like the light of god and the light of thinking shadows over everything. That is a good way to describe the sesshin. Sensory deprivation is another way to describe long meditation. However, it may be better described as a total surrender to god. Everything inside your head, which includes fun, pleasure, dreaming, memories, and imagination, are sacrificed on the alter and all that will remain is a pure mind. Intuition then leads and guides you. Then the world has another saint.

4. DANGERS OF MEDITATION

1. Wrong motive, like wanting to become a karate champion, charismatic leader, psychic, or magician. Those are self glory motives.

2. "Focusing on nothing, or nothingness, can cause possession". The master DK made that statement, but I haven't as yet confirmed it. However, there may be some truth to that statement, because focusing on nothing creates a vacuum. Another entity can then enter the absent self.

The subject of nothing is of interest to meditators, because the outer World and outer self disappears during deep meditation. Then there seems to be nothing left. But something does exist beyond the World of atoms. It's energy.

Surrendering yourself can also create a vacuum. Some seekers surrender all they have to a guru, and then become a mindless follower. That's one way of doing it, but a guru's job is to be a teacher that helps you find the right attitude. If there's something wrong with the guru, then find another one. Keep on guru hopping, and eventually you'll discover that the ultimate guru is within.

3. Combining fasting with meditation seems like a good idea, but it doesn't work. The reason being that meditation requires mental energy to keep the focus going. Without brain sugar, the mind can't concentrate.

4. The kundalini is an energy that moves rapidly up the spine after enlightenment. The movement feels very strong as Spirit cuts an energy channel from the tip of the spine to the top of head. If the movement is natural, then a safe, and healthful stimulation occurs. However, some Yogis have a dangerous practice that pushes energy up the spine. The exercise also cuts a channel up the spine, but the cut is not the same. Back pains, illness, and an uncomfortably high sensitivity may appear which can last for years. A rush of energy is all you'll get when doing it the Yogi way.

The kundalini rush sounds great, but it's **not** a pleasurable high. Neither is it as glorious as many envision it to be. The enlightenment rush will lessen over a couple of days or even a few weeks, and then it's not noticed anymore.

5.   Focusing on chakras can create health problems. The problem is that energy follows thought, and focusing on a chakra increases energy in that chakra. That makes the chakra's endocrine gland squirt out more hormones. The hormones are stimulating, and feel good, but hormones can also create too much growth in the area served by the chakra. As a result, inflammation and cancer may appear. Another problem is, prolonged focusing on the 3rd eye chakra can cause headaches, tunnel vision, and sinus problems.

Chakras are like buttons of energy located about an inch outside of the body. The buttons are composed of spiritual energy, but chakra energy is not the same as your Spirit or soul energy. So not much can be gained by focusing on chakras. Chakras are not the White Light of God.

6. Breathing exercises can also create excess energy, and lead to health problems. Everyone thinks that lots of energy is a good thing, but more health problems are caused by excess energy, then by a lack of it.

7.   Beginners may experience energy problems due to the soul glowing brighter. The increased energy feels good, but it can be exciting. Some beginners will run to and fro with lots of new ideas.

They talk fast, and their mind is racing at 500 miles an hour. They get little sleep and become exhausted, nervous, irritable, or depressed. If that happens, then stop meditating, or reduce the time.

8.   Energy shifts can also happen. Beginners may sometimes get intestinal problems, due to having lots of energy flowing from the belly up to the Heart. That feels good in the Heart, but not so good in the tummy. If lost belly energy is creating distress, then place the hands over the belly. Eating less, or meditating less, may also help.

Another problem happens when deeply contemplating for long periods of time. Excess energy may concentrate in the head, which can cause headaches, and eye problems. If that happens, then switch to the peaceful and safe breath following practice.

9.   Visualizations should be mentioned, because this practice has a good and bad side. A lot of New Age religions use visualizations in their church services to send peace, love, and healing energy to friends, hospitals, pets, etc. Doing it during a church service is safe and good. However, I knew a person that entered a program, which taught her how to become a psychic channel. She did lots of visualizations on angels and masters. A few months

later, she was communicating with space aliens. A couple months after that, she was locked up in a psyche ward. I met her about 6 months after being released, and she was a hyper sensitive mess. It took another 6 months to become fairly normal again. What she didn't know is that visualizations weaken the brain and nervous system by sending body energy to someone **out there**. So limit the visualizations to church services. Also, don't visualize during meditation, because the objective is to make your mind as still as God's Mind.

5. LONG MEDITATIONS

Meditation is learning how to detach from the outer self, so as to become the soul. A long meditation is for learning how to remain in the Mind of Spirit. The body becomes purer and more radiant with each passing day of a long meditation. When the radiance is bright enough, then the aura will catch the eye of your master. He may then decide that it's time for you to join the Brotherhood by granting enlightenment.

Buddhism provides a service for those wishing to take it to the extreme. I stayed at a Zendo which does a 7 day sesshin, twice a year. Some Zendos do it every month. A sesshin is 10 hours of meditation a day for 7 days. That sounds rough, but the rules of the game were the toughest part. During those 7 days, we were not allowed to talk to anyone, except the Roshi, A Roshi is similar to the way a bishop or cardinal is above a priest in a christian church. A Roshi oversees the sesshin. No talking sounds like a strange rule, but some Catholic monasteries allow no talking at all from the day a monk arrives until the day he leaves. Zendos normally allow talking during the morning meeting and work hours. Whispering is allowed the rest of the time. Nobody likes to whisper, so the place is usually quiet. The no talking rule is necessary for learning how to switch attention away from the lights of memory, and over to the Spirit's lights of Love and Mind.

The second rule is that you're not to look anyone in the eye, because a lot of information can be exchanged when doing it. This is supposed to be a time of silence and seclusion. The other rules were,- there is to be **no** reading, writing, radios, TV, or playing musical instruments. Those activities keep attention focused on the outer World. Running and exercising are also prohibited, as desire is the driver of muscles. All of these prohibitions leave you with nothing to do. All escapes have been eliminated.

Boredom can get to be a problem during a long meditation, because the ego isn't having any fun. Fortunately, the ego and its' boredom problem disappears when consciousness is centered in God's Mind. It's because your Spirit and soul are more interested in Life itself.

The worst thing about a long meditation is you might not achieve enlightenment. Only six out of twenty two made it during the one I attended, and one of those was sitting her 10th sesheen. The second and third days were the toughest, due to sitting still for 10 hours a day. After that, life became more beautiful with each passing day. I still see the 7 day sesheen as being the highest point of my life.

A few years later, I sat a Tibetan dahtun, which is 30 days of meditation at 10 hours a day. That sounds really rough, but it was actually easier. No drugs or alcohol were the only rules. 70 of us sat the dahtun in the Colorado Mountains, and it became the most beautiful time of my life. A deep Love connected all of us, and being allowed to talk helped us learn how to relate soul to soul.

Higher spirituality can only be achieved by discarding the frontside character, and becoming the peaceful, humble soul. The way to get there is to be still and know god. Getting there means sitting perfectly still, no thinking, and no internal talking. Then awareness will move from the active front side to the rear half of the head and spine. Those areas have the biggest concentrations of nerves. That's important to know because the soul is half light of spirit, and half nervous system. The technique is to silence the front side's desire, pride, emotions, and imagining. Then attention will turn rearward to the peaceful soul. The longer attention remains looking rearward, the brighter spirit becomes. When the light of spirit becomes bright enough, then your master will give the gift of enlightenment. You are then a soul man, a Son of god. The next task is to remain that way. That's hard to do because almost everyone you meet and know is a human animal. So let it be known that inner and outer silence is essential to being the soul.

6. BEST TIME TO MEDITATE

Meditation can be done at any time of the day or night. It can even be done at work. Difficult problems can be solved by entering into a deep contemplative mode. Almost any time is a good time to meditate, except when at a party. It's best to meditate right after awakening, because you have been unconscious for the last 8 hours. The emotions and desires are still sluggish, so making those placid is easy to do. Nothing happens during sleep, other than an occasional dream, so there are seldom any memories to spark off thoughts. That makes it a lot easier to enter the still Mind of Spirit.

Consciousness gets started off right by meditating in the morning, because the divine peacefulness will stick with you throughout the day. Happenings that normally irritate you will just bounce off. Others can be going through their hysterical dramas, but it doesn't faze you. All it takes is 30 minutes of meditating in the morning to make the day much nicer.

Two to 4AM is when spirituality is at its' peak, but tiredness will usually ruin a 2AM meditation.

The best time is shortly before dawn, like 5 or 6AM. A cup of tea before meditating works well. So does the juice of a freshly squeezed lemon.

Two to 4 in the afternoon is when spirituality is at its' lowest. That's because sunlight stimulates the brain and nervous system. Two photons of sunlight creates an electron, and the high afternoon energy makes it harder to get past the outer self. However, don't think that daytime meditations should be eliminated. We meditated at the Zendo before each meal, and it was surprising to see the amount of tenseness created by just 3 hours of work. Another advantage is better digestion.

Sundown is the next best time to meditate, but attention has been focused outward for about the last 10 hours. Memories of what happened during the day are now sparking off thoughts. However, the nice thing about an evening meditation is the peacefulness produced before bedtime creates a better nights sleep. Try watching the breath, after getting in bed, and you'll quickly drop off to a nice deep sleep.

Spiritual learning can be accelerated by living in a meditation center. It's a "birds of a feather flock together" thing. Everyone is interested in higher spirituality, and lots of spiritual experiences are heard. However, getting to live in a meditation center is usually a problem, because most of the centers are full. They may have a waiting list, but there's only a small chance that you'll ever be called. So plan B is to meditate at home. That works well, because lots of social mistakes have to be made before getting your act right. And most of those mistakes are made at home or work.

Spiritual growth can be increased by reading spiritual books. I recommend reading the Alice Bailey book of Ponder On This. It's a compilation of what the ascended master DK said on 186 subjects. DK has an intuitive style of writing, so it's best to read his books after meditating. That's when your mind is more open and intuitive.

7. RELAXATION

We were never interested in learning how to relax during childhood, because back then, life was all about doing things, and having fun. Now that we are older, and more tired, it's time to learn how to conserve energy by relaxing. Better health then follows.

What will eventually be learned is that you can remain relaxed all day long, and perform just as well as when speedy. In many cases better, because the mind is clearer, and fewer mistakes are being made.

Relaxation is the first meditation practice to learn, because relaxation **detaches** awareness from the body, desires, and emotions. That's the first step in gaining higher spirituality, and it's a very important one. Try spending the first 8 hours practicing the different relaxation techniques.

There are 3 relaxation practices to master. The first one is to make the muscles feel warm and heavy. This practice works best for detaching from desire, because the muscles are controlled by desire. First feel the face and say,- my face feels warm and heavy. Next feel the neck and say,- my neck feels warm and heavy. Go through all of the muscles making them feel warm and heavy. Next time, shorten it to just the big parts, like the head, arms, legs, and torso. After that, shorten it to just the upper body and lower body. Finally, shorten it to,- my whole body feels warm and heavy. The whole body then relaxes in just one second. This is the best practice for learning how to remain relaxed all day long, every day.

The second practice is focusing on the sinking feeling of the outgoing breath. Feel the upper body sink with each outgoing breath. This practice works well for quickly switching consciousness to the inner self.

The sinking technique also works well for falling asleep. Feel the body sink into the bed with each outgoing breath, and you'll quickly fall off to a nice deep sleep.

The third relaxation practice is breath counting. Count each outgoing breath all the way to the end. Say oonnne, twoooo, threeee, etc, all the way up to 10. Then start over again at one. This practice was given to me when entering the Zendo. We were expected to always start a meditation by breath counting. Breath counting works best before starting a contemplation practice, because it automatically focuses attention on the 3rd eye. Breath counting also works best when feeling overly stimulated, scared, angry, or emotional. Relaxation is the most important spiritual practice this is how you change from human to god. Try spending the whole meditation relaxing. There are 1000 practices to focus on, and what you'll eventually discover is that focusing on deep breath with relaxation works best. Human consciousness dips below cravings, pleasure, pride, Brain imaginings, dreams, possessions, and things. You become the lowest thing on earth. Then it becomes obvious that " the lowest are the highest" according to Jesus.

Relaxation is like the foundation of higher spirituality, so don't skip lightly over this lesson. Learn how to remain relaxed all day, every day. Check the body a dozen times a day to see if it is relaxed. After the body is able to remain relaxed, then work on relaxing the brain, so as to become mentally peaceful. That requires learning meditation. This can be learned at home. The magical sound use MU, HU, or UU mantra. This sound helps to return attention back to the center of the head, where god's mind is located, and then you will know peace.

8. POSTURES

Some teachers insist on everyone sitting in the full lotus posture. There's some truth to that, because meditation is better when the body is more compact. Seekers in India, Japan, and other Eastern countries find it easy to get into the full lotus posture, because it's customary for them to sit on the floor. But here in the West, we sit on chairs. As a result, the ligaments and muscles are usually too tight for the full lotus. The muscles also become tighter as we age, so looser postures are needed for seniors.

Meditating while standing has the problem of walking away. Meditating while lying down has the problem of falling asleep. What's left is sitting. Any of the sitting postures will do, however, it's best to find one that's comfortable. Leg pains are the biggest problem for any age group. If the legs hurt, then try a looser version of the lotus posture. Uncross a leg, and put it out front. A more comfortable posture is to put both feet out front. If leg pains persist, then move the feet out farther. The ankles can be crossed, or uncrossed. The bottoms of the feet can be touching, or apart. However, if the feet are way out front, then stability gets to be a problem. That can be corrected by putting a pillow behind the lower back, and leaning against a wall. Sitting on a chair is the last option, however, a chair may work better for seniors, because they often have knee or circulation problems. Try all of the different ways to find the one that works best for you.

The tailor posture works best for some. The word tailor comes from the way tailors, in the 1800's, would sit while sewing. They sat on their feet, or on a big pillow. A large pillow is needed, for both the tailor and lotus postures, to raise the butt off the floor about 4 inches. Then the spine becomes "straight", which is a natural S curve. When the spine is straight, then it's easy to sit upright and be comfortable. The final part is balancing the head on the shoulders.

The hands are to be resting comfortably in the lap. The usual way is to place the fingers of one hand on the fingers of the other. Don't interlock the fingers, as that will eventually cause finger pains. The hands can also be positioned with the finger tips touching, or they can be apart about 3 inches, so as to square the shoulders. That's an important point, because chest pains may happen, during a long meditation, due to the shoulders being slightly slumped. The hands can also be placed on the knees, if there's knee pain.

If there is discomfort in the belly, then place the hands across the belly. The hands can be resting on the belt, so as to keep them at belly level. Another way is to fold the shirt around the hands, so as to form a sling that is at belly level.

A famous posture is placing the hands on the knees with the palms up. The idea is to receive energy from God, or some other divine entity out there. That is hocus pocus. The divine energy you want is radiating from within, so don't try to suck energy from the sky.

The eyes are to be open a slit, and gazing at a place on the floor about 3 feet away. The eyes appear to be closed, but the lower part of the room can be dimly seen. It's hard for beginners to keep the eyes open a little, but the problem goes away after about 10 hours of practice. One advantage of keeping the eyes open a little is the mind doesn't dream as much. Another advantage is the eyes need to be slightly open when becoming the detached observer.

Discomfort can ruin a good meditation. Use a blanket if necessary to get cozy, and warm. Move the legs to a different position if they hurt. Slap the bothersome mosquito. Do whatever is needed to become comfortable. Sounds can still be heard, but ignore the sounds. Finally, don't move a muscle. Sit perfectly still, so as to detach from the body. Sitting still for 30 or 40 minutes may sound hard to do, but it's easy.

Buddhists have a solution for leg pains. They do a slow 5 minute walk every half hour. Someone rings a bell, and everyone stands up. A line is formed, and everyone walks slowly around the room. Some clasp their hands on the chest, in a devotional manner, while most will clasp their hands across the belly. The procedure is to walk slow, and watch the feeling of the feet touching the floor. Then a meditator remains mindful of what they are doing, which is just walking.

Start a meditation by getting in your favorite posture, and then lean way forward. That stretches the back muscles, and makes attention look at the backside. Then arch the spine forward as you slowly sit up, however, remain focused on the upper back while sitting up. A meditation will get off to a faster start when attention is on the upper backside.

It's because the front side's emotions and desires are being ignored.

The lights should be low, so the mind isn't being stimulated by light. Low lights work well during the morning meditation, but drowsiness can become a problem during the evening meditation. So the light level needs to be a little higher in the evening.

Set aside an area for meditating. If there's no place to sit, then part of the bed can be used. After that, meditate in the same space every day. The reason being that it's easier to become the soul, when the space is already saturated with your energy. That sounds magical, but there's something to it. I could always feel a strong energy when entering the Zendo's meditation room. It was as noticeable as walking from the hot outdoors into a cool room. Three years later, I was sitting a 30 day Tibetan dahtun, and the cook said that he was having fun sitting on the pillows of others during the meditation breaks. He claimed that, "some pillows were extremely peaceful, while others had lots of power".

Keeping the eyes opened just a slit it is hard to do, but is important. The soul is a detached observer, or should I say, an observer who was very detached. It can also be said that detached observer is your souls personality. Or like it is a primary part of the soul's personality. This practice helps to see what your mind is doing. It is supposed to be only looking forward, but the child prefers to be looking at desires, and proud imaginings, feelings, emotional dramas, or listing to the verbal ego's talking, or imagination's pictures. Attention could also be focused on intellectual possibilities and memories, or creating stories. Awareness of all these mental interruptions helps to create self awareness that in turn helps to create thought control.

9. MANTRAS

Mantras are sounds, and sound is energy. Different sounds create different feelings, as you already know by the many feelings produced by music. Mantras are usually single sounds, however some can be as long as a sentence, such as the OM MANI PADME HUM. This mantra came from India, and is composed of 4 sacred words. What's comical about it is a belief that your wishes will come true, if the mantra is repeated over and over. Interestingly enough, there are lots of intelligent people actually doing it in hopes of making their wishes come true. That is another hocus pocus belief.

HUM is the sound of the soul. It's pronounced hoom, which rhymes with boom. However, MM is the actual sound of the soul, for it's the sound of the Heart. That's the largest and most radiant of Spirit's energies. There are 2 ways of doing the HUM. One way is to sound it in a relaxing manner, so as to **detach** from the emotions. The other is to sound the HUM in a questioning manner, so as to **detach** from the excited brain.

Start a meditation by first relaxing. Then bow

forward to feel the backside muscles stretch. Sit back up, and silently sound the HUM all the way to the end of the breath. Continue sounding the HUM, UM, or MM until becoming centered in the peaceful Heart. Then you'll know the meaning of divine peacefulness.

The peaceful Heart is a nice place to be, but there are days when the brain won't slow down. So the answer is to do one of the UU mantras. The sound of UU, HU, or MU works well for calming the mind. When the mind is finally still, then you'll know the meaning of mental peacefulness.

The sound of MU is pronounced moo, like a cow says it. This mantra was given to me when entering the Zendo. I was to say MUUUU all the way to the end of the breath. Then think, what is MU? Coupling MU with a question works well, because the soul thinks in a questioning manner. An answer may appear, but who cares? The question was only a vehicle for moving consciousness closer to the intuitive Mind. I refuse to disclose the answer to any Zen koan, or even give out hints. You'll have to do a long meditation at a Zendo to find that answer.

You'll often notice, during meditation, that a dream has just ended. How long attention was distracted by the dream is unknown. It could have been a minute, or maybe even 10 minutes. The dream was fun, but its' remnants have to be cleared away, or the dream will reappear again. The MU, HU, or UU works well for sweeping away dream dust.

OM is the most sacred of the mantras, because it's the sound of Spirit. Almost every seeker has heard of the OM, and tried it, but few know how to properly sound it. The correct way is to sound the OM, and then focus on it vibrating the roof of the mouth. Next, send the vibration up to the brain, so as to connect with Spirit.

Don't get the idea that mantras are magical practices that will make you levitate, or make sparks jump from the finger tips. Also, don't think that you can become enlightened by spending hours sounding the OM. Your master knows what's happening, so that idea won't work. The attitudes of harmlessness, brotherhood, and being the helping hand of God have to be in place before you can change into a Son of God.

Play around with the different mantras to find the ones that work best for you. When the intellect is finally silent, then it's time to discontinue all mantras. That's because generating a sound is disturbing to the stillness of God's Mind.

Sounds are energy. Sounding MM increases energy in the chest. Too much energy in the chest is irritating to the brachials, like when suffering a cold or flu. If that happens then switch to the UU mantras or just watch the outgoing breath touching their nostrils breath following. The UU sound sends energy up to the brain. If a headache in the brain becomes painful, then switch to breath following. That is the safest meditation practice. Too much energy in any part of the body causes pain. This is known as inflammation. Prolonged irritation produces cancer, so be aware of inflammation.

GOD, SPIRIT, & SOUL

10. GOD CHARACTERISTICS

Not much is known about God, except we do know that God is Life. Everything is alive. Even the atoms have life and intelligence. It's an attraction and repulsion type of intelligence that atoms use for joining into little colonies called molecules.

There's a metaphysical piece of logic about God that's intriguing:

"Before the Heavens and Earth were created, there was nothing.

So if out of nothing came something.

Then nothing must be something".

We can only deduce, from the above reasoning, that God must be space and some form of energy.

The master DK claimed that, "God has 7 characteristics. Eternal Love, eternal Mind, and eternal Will to Good, are 3 of them. The masters know about the 4th, but that's it". Can you imagine that. Mankind's most spiritually intelligent don't have a clue about the other 3 forms of God. So don't get in a fight over beliefs about God. Getting in a fight sounds ridiculous, but actual wars have been fought over religious beliefs.

God is said to be infinite, so what is infinite? Lets use numbers to define it. 999,999,999,999,999,999,999,999,999,999,999,999 ,999 is a really big number, but it's not yet infinite. If we continued making 9's all the way to the wall, it would still not be infinite. If we continued making 9s all the way to the moon, it would still not be infinite. We can only describe infinity as going on and on forever. Now comes the question of how could an infinite God have been born from out of nothing? Apparently, God has to be something that's less than nothing.

The World Religions are wrestling with the question of whether God is immanent or omnipotent. Immanent means that God is within everything, and is controlling all of His creations. Omnipotent, means that God created everything, and then detached from His creations. These theories seem to contradict each other, but the answer is both. Some day, during deep meditation, you'll see that both theories are correct.

God is in this World, yet, He's detached from everything. God allows everyone to be free, but on occasions, God will tempt us. A clue about this is in the Lord's Prayer, which says, "and lead us not into temptation, but deliver us from evil". Jesus was implying that God leads us into temptation. That means Earth is a big school where we have to learn lessons and take tests.

Buddha offered the best advice to anyone trying to figure out what is God. He would tell the devotee to quit thinking about it, and just meditate. That is good advice, because trying to solve the question is like a mouse trying to solve algebra equations. Man's intellectual abilities are puny compared to the intuition. And the intuition is small compared to the Universal Mind. Larger yet is the Cosmic Mind. And there may even be a larger Mind than that out there.

GOD'S LOVE

Love is a big subject. A thousand books have been written about love, but none have been able to fully explain it. Below is a brief outline of Love.

God's Love originates from a tiny point of bright light within the center of the chest. It can be seen (with insight) as a radiant ball of light that's about 3 inches in diameter. This bright light interacts with nerves on the front of the chest to create emotions and affection.

Probationers are able to feel the Love of God radiating from deep within their chest. They become intrigued by the feeling, and often attend church services to increase the radiant feeling. Some even go beyond the beautiful feeling to realizing that they are Love. They instantly know that Love is who they are. It's their real self. This realization can happen during a church service, or during meditation, or in other ways. It happened to me in an 8 hour group therapy session. During the last hour, I was too wasted to even defend my self. That's when I suddenly realized that Love is my true nature. It's who I am. This inner energy had been felt for years, but it never occurred to me that Love is who I am.

Love doesn't think, but a strand of intuition extends from the head down to the Heart. Then Love knows what to say and do. The combination of Love and Mind is called wisdom, or loving understanding. Keep on meditating, and Love will slowly increase in radiance. Eventually, its' radiance will percolate up to the center of the brain, and connect with Mind. Then Love becomes your leader.

Love can be divided into 6 parts.

(1.) Hot sexual or romantic love. Sex creates a feeling of Oneness with another, and the two become soul mates. They feel so united that they'll arrange a marriage ceremony to tell the World about their love for each other. They feel God's eternal Love, and know that their union will last forever. That's why sex is sacred. (2.) Warm affectionate love is like the nurturing, protective love of a mother towards her baby. This form of love is something that women have in abundance. Their bodies give warm milk to babies, and they give lots of warm affectionate love to something that just lies there. Motherly love can be seen in all of the species of nature from birds to elephants. Even the crocodiles have it. Affectionate love can also be fatherly, brotherly, sisterly, grandmotherly, or grandfatherly.

(3.) God's Love is magnetic. It holds society together by a magnetism called unity, or brotherhood. This magnetism can be felt at meetings where there's a common effort, such as with labor unions, or church services. Unity can also be felt by members of a team, tribe, community, nation, etc. Fortunately for humanity,

Nations are slowly unifying as they meet at the United Nations to discuss their differences. Even the World religions are unifying; as priests are slowly realizing that all religions have two things in common. It's God's Love and Goodness.

(4.) Benevolent love is the helping hand. This is where many are focused from charity volunteers to those performing individual acts of loving kindness. Some even devote their life to helping others.

(5.) Compassionate love is the Love of All. This is a loving connection with the Hearts of all beings, from humans to worms.

(6.) Oneness is a good way to describe God's Love. It's a Oneness of everything from atoms to plants, animals, people, Planets, Suns, and Galaxies. The Oneness of All becomes known at enlightenment when pure Love connects with pure Mind. Then it's obvious that everyone is a divine being, and heaven does exist on Earth.

GOD'S MIND

God's Mind originates from a tiny point of bright light located in the center of the brain. Its' radiance creates a ball of light called intuition. This light creates a high, wide, deep, and clear way of mentally seeing. The intuition has a "to see is to know" way of thinking. It sees the big picture, or the greater whole. Then everything about the subject is obvious.

The intuition's way of mentally seeing is like being high up on a mountain, and seeing the grand vista. Intuition looks at the whole scene, whereas the outer mind has a tunnel vision way of seeing. It looks at just one part of the scene at a time. Such as, the intellect focuses on just that mountain, and then on just that valley. There's more on intuition in chapter 22.

GOD'S GOODNESS, or WILL to GOOD

God's Goodness is also called God's Will to Good, God's Power, or God's Will. This energy radiates from a ball of light located at the tail of the spine. Some of it moves up the front side to create hard headed will power, and feelings of honor. However, all of it goes up the spine,after enlightenment happens. The ultra strong feeling of energy flowing up the spine is called kundalini energy.

Only a tiny amount God's Power is allotted to humans, because it can be easily converted into hard hearted and hard headed will power. Human will power seems to have lots of strength, but it's small when compared to the soul's Will Power, and puny when compared to God's Will Power.

Divine Goodness energy feels like God's helpful attitude. It inspires people to help others, and volunteer to do good deeds. The energy also inspires everyone to end their bad habits, and become a better person.

Everyone's path is littered with discarded things

that were once precious, but are now useless. Such as, probationers are discarding their physical pleasures. Mystics are discarding their emotional pleasures, and contemplators are discarding their imagination pleasures. A "second death" is experienced when desire stops driving the outer self. God's Power then has to become the pusher of everything said, thought, and done. That's because Love only attracts, and Mind only sees. If Divine Power was absent, then nothing would get done.

Enlightenment is something like an internship, where more needs to be learned, and tough tests lie ahead. A Son of God has almost no outer self left, and is given more of God's Power. However, the amount remains small, because he is not yet totally trustworthy. Such as, a Son of God may try using his divine Power to control others. That seems like a good idea, for good works can then be accomplished. But everyone needs to remain free, so as to make some stupid mistakes, and learn more lessons. Eventually, a Son of God will graduate from the "Halls of Wisdom". Then he's trustworthy enough to be given more of God's Power.

This is as far as I dare to go. The year 4000 is when more knowledge about God's Power can be imparted. But a common man will never be trustworthy enough to know how to use God's Power. It would be like giving a razor blade to a small child.

THE INNER SPIRIT

God is Life. God's lively energy must be present for a body to breathe, and be active. God's Life Force is composed of 3 strings of light that extend from the tail of the spine to the top of the head. Then the strings go out the top of the head to somewhere unknown.

The strings of Spirit are like 3 strands of a fiber optic cable. The strands are thin, and a tiny bright light shines from the end of each strand. That creates the 3 radiant spheres of Spirit, as illustrated on the front cover.. One strand ends in the center of the head. Another ends in the spiritual Heart, and a third ends at the tip of the spine.

SOUL Spirit's personality.

Spirit is so detached that an in between consciousness is needed to connect Spirit with matter, and soul is that consciousness. The soul is aware of both the outer World, and its inner Spiritual energies. That's how the soul got to be your inner guide.

Soul consciousness is like Spirit's personality; in that the soul is created by the radiance of Spirit's Love, Goodness, and Mind. The soul's role is to be aware of the outer, and learn how to do things the right way. It has to patiently watch and learn many painful lessons during a thousand lifetimes on Earth. A million mistakes will be made, but mistakes are good, because pain and bad memories create understanding.

The soul's job is to help the outer self, but the proud ego prefers to do things its way. So the detached soul has to patiently watch and wait while the outer self pursues its pleasures, treasures, and happiness. Those activities eventually get to be old, and most of the funster has disappeared by the age of 30. Then the soul becomes more noticeable, and religion is more interesting.

The radiance of God's Love is felt deep within the chest of probationers. The wonderful feeling creates a desire to spread the word about God's Love. Evangelism is thus born. Then on a higher level is the enlightenment experience. That's when a seeker changes from connecting with his soul to **being** his soul. The experience is so fantastic that enlightened ones also feel a need to spread the word. They want everyone to meditate and become enlightened. Buddhism defines these people as bodhisattvas. "A being that compassionately refrains from entering nirvana, so as to save others". But in both cases, the evangelists and bodhisattvas eventually get used to their wonderful feelings. The desire to spread the word slows down, and attention turns more inward. Evangelists become interested in the soul's peacefulness, and bodhisattvas become interested in Spirit's energies. The desire to have others experience what they feel is just a phase.

11. SOUL CHARACTERISTICTICS

1.Compassion, or comradely passion--- God's Love is best described as Oneness, which is a sympathetic feeling with all beings. Compassion feels the suffering of others, and strives to relieve their suffering. Compassion extends to the Hearts of all living beings, such as, seeing a starving dog evokes an impulse to help the poor thing.

There's another form of compassion known as heroism. That's when a person puts his life in danger to save another from death or injury. In a lot of cases, the hero didn't even know the person he saved. That is illogical behavior, but the soul knows the importance of keeping life going as long as possible.

2. Wisdom---Zen Buddhism got it right, for they tell the seekers to make wisdom their goal. That means being centered in the Heart, and thinking with loving understanding (**wisdom**). The Heart seems to think, but in reality, Love doesn't think. A chord of intuition extends from the center of the brain down to the Heart. Then Love knows what to say and do.

The soul's loving understanding has a social intelligence, or an ability to know what to say, and when to say it. It also knows when not to say it. There have been times when I have said something from the Heart, and later concluded that it was a mistake. Something happened the next day, and I then realized that it was the perfect thing to say.

Perfect timing is another interesting thing about wisdom. This is a psychic knowing of when to do something, and when **not** to do something. What's equally intriguing is Love's ability to know what's in the Hearts of others. All Hearts are connected, because all come from the same source. So knowing what's in the Hearts of others helps to find the perfect thing to say and do. Women, on average, have a higher social intelligence, and more of Love's psychic ability. It's due to being more centered in their Heart. That creates a wiser, kinder, and more caring personality. Most men catch up after 40.

3. Intuitive and psychic--- Soul consciousness

is when a meditator becomes a detached observer. His outer mind is completely placid, and everything is now obvious. That's when he thinks by **intuitively knowing**.

A soul man is able think with the intellect, if he wants to, but the soul prefers to remain centered in the intuitive Mind. That's because it's easier to **intuitively** and **psychically know things** than to grind away with the intellect. The intuition just knows things; even though there are no facts to back it up. It's that simple.

The intuition also gives out psychic information. Humans think that psychism is something unusual and fascinating, but what they don't know is that it's natural to be psychic. Even the animals are psychic. The problem humans have is their intellect blocks them from being psychic. When the spotlight stops focusing on the imagination and intellect, then the intuition has to take over. The intuition doesn't think. It knows, and some of the knowledge is called psychic phenomena.

You may wonder, what is it like to be centered in the soul. Enlightenment is like the first time it happened to me. The enlightenment experience. The first half hour is where lots of spirit's light is experienced, and God's world is seen. See chapter one. After that it feels like being in a different world, and in the mother's Earth's world at the same time. A day later this sesshin ended. Those who became enlightened remained solidly peaceful and quiet. All the other 14 became talkative and happy. Some were a little crazy. The next day I had to go into town. The people I met seemed like children. It seemed like I could see them, but they couldn't see me. Another deep soul experience happened after fasting two days when the Moon was in Taurus. Once again it felt like I was "in this world but not of it," as Jesus said. The friends I were riding with, and almost every one around seemed like 10 or 12 year old children. While standing in the checkout line, I wondered how much will these items cost, and the answer came back $55.00. The cashier rang up the items and the price was $55.00. We went to one other store and again I asked myself how much will this cost. The answer came back as $37.00, and the cashier also rang up $37.00. The soul thinks with God's mind.

4. Joy--- God is the great helper that helps everyone in the World. The Heart glows after helping someone, because the act was pleasing God. The beautiful glow is called joy. It's God's reward for helping others. A different form of joy happens when Hearts meet, like at a communal fellowship, or a family get-together. And another form of joy happens when falling in love.

Happiness is different than joy. Happiness is created by things made of atoms, such as, food, money, and possessions. The days of childhood are when we had lots of fun running, skipping, and playing games. Then around the age of 12, we became interested in pleasure. Prudent people will say that pleasure is bad, but there's a different side to it. The reason why sex, drugs, and alcohol makes you feel so good is partly because the energy of joy is being released.

Only the mountain tops of joy were hit, but this will suffice. A whole book could be written about it.

5.   **Devotion**--- "To that for which we live". Devotion is usually thought of as kneeling, praying, and following a spiritual teacher, but you can also be devoted to your spouse, children, job, group, church, community, or nation. Devotion is Love's readiness to help.

6. Purity--- Becoming a Pure Being happens when detaching from the outer self, and outer World. Then all that remains is the pure Heart and Mind of soul.

The radiance of the Pure One within creates a drive for purity and perfection. Some take the feeling of purity to the extreme by fasting. Some bathe 3 times a day, while others insist on wearing white clothes, and drinking purified water. These practices are for purifying the physical self. But it's more important to purify yourself of desires, emotions, and imaginings.

The evangelists tell about being reborn, and pure as a baby again, when they accept Jesus as their savior. The enlightened ones also tell about being purified at enlightenment. Then a higher purity happens when seeing a tiny point of bright light. The feeling is something like bathing in white light, for the body feels completely clean and new again.

Whether or not to mention the tiny point of bright light is debatable, because 11% of the schizophrenics think they are Jesus. Unfortunately, some of the insane will become spiritual teachers, and some day, an insane teacher will invent a point of light meditation practice. Then he'll claim that it can make everyone see the tiny point of bright light.

Don't believe it. Seekers need to know about this phenomena, and yet know that it's way beyond their present schooling. A long meditation is needed to become enlightened. After that, another long meditation is needed to experience the tiny point of bright light. That's a lot to go through just to experience the ultimate in purity.

Many seekers feel the purity of their soul, and some become obsessed with purifying the outer self. Some develop strange ways of doing it, like a fellow that joined the Zendo. He expelled lots of gas all day long. When asked about the problem, he explained that it was a spiritual practice. He was "gulping in lots of air, so as to fart it out the other end. That purified his innards of foul odors". Needless to say, he was quickly booted from the Zendo.

Extremism is common for those on the path. Such as, Jesus and Buddha took purification practices to the extreme. Jesus fasted for 40 days, and then started his ministry. Buddha sat under a tree and meditated for 40 days. During that time, he would eat only the fruits that fell from trees. Meditation was widely practiced during Buddha's time, but nobody knew that a long meditation would result in enlightenment. That happened to

Buddha on the 40th day.

I can't criticize anyone for taking spirituality to the extreme, because I did lots of 3 and 7 day fasts. The idea was to purify my body of toxins, but I eventually learned that a 3 day fast did more than that. My mind was completely clear upon awakening on the 4th morning. I could see forever, and questions that had me stumped were answered within a second. Years later, I learned that fasting wasn't necessary to reach those high peaks. Pure Mind can be reached during a morning meditation, and good health can be had by eating a low calorie diet. Consuming less than 1,000 calories a day renews the cells mitochondria. It's also a relief to the internal organs. Two weeks later, the body returns to good health.

Purity is an important step in consciousness. It's more like the last mile of the spiritual path. We go from pure being to light being (adept). Enlightenment is halfway from pure being to light being. Evolving from human being to pure being can be summed up in one word – feelings. Almost all of humanity is obsessed with their feelings. The biggest error made is with confusing the light of spirit with spiritual feelings created by alcohol, marijuana, heroin, cocaine, meth, and sex. Spiritual feelings are not spiritually, It feels that way, but indulging in those substances and feelings are defined as sinfulness. Where people go wrong is they are very focused and attached to their feelings. That has to be eliminated before enlightenment can happen. Being cold hearted it is not the way to eliminate feelings. Meditation and lots of self awareness will diminish feelings, so as to become the peaceful soul. Detachment is absolutely necessary, so as a space of "I am in the world but not of it". Here's something to think about. Master DK claims that masters have no pain and feel no pain because they have no feelings.

Pure MM is soul mind. Getting to that high peak means discarding your human nature. Start out by getting rid of the painful emotions of anger, fear, sadness, and shame. Lots of self study is needed. Eliminate those emotions from consciousness. The next one to eliminate is party spirit, cravings for marijuana, cocaine, meth, alcohol, heroin and anything else. The brain produces a chemical called dopamine. Once the love of party drugs has ended, then the brain can turn inward for another dopamine eye on daydreaming. A lot more soul studying is needed to produce the self awareness needed to conquer the daydreaming addiction. The beauty of self awareness is you can see what the ego is doing to have fun. Meditation is absolutely needed for this path, because daydreams become very obvious when they interrupt a meditation. When the outer mind can be held clearer and more steady, then pure mind is achieved. The next step is to do a long meditation, so as to become enlightened. The final step in evolving from human beings to pure being a is to do another long meditation. That is the end of traveling on earth. Ascended master is the next step, but that has to happen in god's world.

Fasting is a super tool for cleaning out the mental debris, and making it easy to hold the wild mind steady. Three day fasts work best for seekers. The first day is easy. Hunger is not much of a problem, and a lot of strength is available. Fatigue sets in and hunger on the second day. Fatigue gets in on the third day but hunger starts to fade away. Morning of the fourth day is when it is clear, and answers to long held questions are instantly answered by intuition. End the fast slowly with juices and easy to stomach foods, like fruit, potatoes, and artichokes. All that's needed during a fast is cold water. However, I am 83 and decided that some nutrients would be helpful. So I take

DHEA and CoQ10, which is a heart energy nutrient. That's taken in the AM. Before bedtime, another CoQ10, plus melatonin for sleeping is taken. If pain or discomfort is present at bedtime, then I take an ibuprofen. Pepto Bismol and creatinine work well during a fast. Pills also.

Pure heart pure mind, the most valuable mantra for seekers are then UM, HU, and HUM. MM is the sound of the soul. This sound works best when trying to become deeply peaceful by the practice of breath following. At some point, the peaceful seeker becomes pure heart. The UU sound calms a wild brain. HU or UU works best. At some point the seeker will become pure mind. HU also works best when a dream interrupts the meditation. The fastest way to get back is to breath count up to 4 or 5 and then start sounding UU again.

7. Humbleness Souls, adepts, and masters have no self image, and see themselves as being just ordinary people. They are servants of all, and there's nothing great about being a servant. As a result, "the lowest are the highest", according to Jesus.

The humbleness being referred to is not the humbling of defeat, or the humbleness of a penniless beggar. Humans want to be something great, while seekers are heading towards being nothing. Seekers instinctively know that they have to become nothing in order to become something. Everything about the ego has to disappear in order to become the divine soul. Once there, then the humbleness feels natural.

Most try to establish superiority, and then maintain it. However, old age manages to change everything. Competing to establish physical superiority has to end, because the old muscles have lost their endurance. Mental superiority is also lost as the mind becomes slower and foggier. The beauty of a young body is lost to fat, wrinkles, and gray hair. We lose just about everything during old age, but that's good, because it humbles us back to being natural.

We think of pleasure as being created by outer things, like sex, drugs, and music, but pleasure can also be created in the brain. Dreams of greatness and self-goodness can inflate the self image way up to the splendor of glory. But when pride's greatness and glory is deflated way down to nothing, then the self image is destroyed. That is depressing, but the highly evolved find that it's comforting to be a humble nobody. It feels like the fight is finally over.

Desire drives the body to move, talk, and think. Another strong driver is the imagination. Self image creates the personality, and imagined position on the ladder of success. Falling off the self image ladder can result in months of deep depression. I fell all the way off the ladder when awakening one morning to find that I was blind. It was caused by a diabetic retinopathy. Too much sugar and sweets created this problem. Fortunately I could still see a little bit out of the lower corner of the right eye. I was close to the self image ladder, so it wasn't much of a fall, however, I was now down to the very bottom. It meant relying on others just to survive. Others have to read ton me, drive to the store, find items, and repair possessions. My eyes have strengthened, driving the last couple of years, however it feels nice to be equal to penniless beggars and homeless dogs. Falling off the ladder of self importance and success is a good thing. When mental stimulants like coffee, drugs, money, and possessions disappear, then reality returns. That's when the insanity of society becomes noticeable. Being humble is natural, but few ever get that low.

8.   Responsible--- I was once a member of the

military. One day, the master sergeant announced that we were to have some kind of paperwork done by tomorrow, and he didn't want any excuses. Naturally, I messed up and didn't do it, so I had to face him. He asked, "Why didn't you get this done". I was stunned for about 5 seconds, and finally answered, "no excuse sir". That was hard to do. I couldn't hide behind lies and excuses like children do. I had to step forward, and stand with the courageous ones. It took only 5 seconds for me to grow up. The sergeant smiled and signed the paper. That was a life changing experience.

There's an outer responsibility of supplying the needs of yourself and family. Then there's an inner responsibility of being responsible for everything said, thought, and done. That's when probationers start to clean up their act, and live in truth. A deeper responsibility is felt when connecting with the Hearts of all beings. Then seekers choose to become the helping hand of God.

9. Harmlessness--- It means being verbally, physically, and mentally harmless. Harming others is wrong. The exception being when having to protect yourself from aggressive people, animals, or insects.

Mother Earth radiates lots of Love and Goodness, and heaven does exist on Earth. Unfortunately, Earth is infested with cruelty. Animals fight for territory. Even the beautiful butterflies fight for territory. The human kingdom is worse in that havoc can be created on a large scale, like when nations fight nations. Desire, superiority, and arrogance are behind most of the cruelty on Earth.

I bought a BB gun at the age of 12. I loved shooting it, but I eventually became tired of shooting only at targets. The solution was to be a hunter. I killed some birds, frogs, and gophers, but afterwards, there never was a good feeling. Something within me also died. I later bought a 22, and continued to hunt. But it seemed as though the bigger the animal killed, the worse I felt. Then one day I watched a rabbit die, and that was it. The feeling was so bad that I finally quit hunting. Later on, I noticed that a good feeling was experienced whenever I helped wildlife. Feeding birds, gophers, and other wildlife made me feel more alive. It turns out that all living beings on Earth are also students in God's School of Life. All are entitled to life, liberty, and learning. So needlessly harming anything is wrong.

Harming others seems to be natural, because

children grow up in an environment where "might makes right". That makes many conclude that they have the right to do whatever they want toward others of lesser size, strength, and wealth. Unfortunately, the only thing that an ignorant child can do is copy his parents cruel ways. And what was learned during childhood is retained throughout life. So the solution is to do a self study on cruelty. Many will find it is still appearing in their thoughts, talk, and secret feelings.

Harmlessness is an excellent way to become healthier, for a purer attitude towards others helps to clean and purify the body. A vegetarian diet is an absolute must for anyone wanting to become enlightened, because destroying the Hearts of others is wrong. We need to eat something, and plants are here to help us. Plants breathe carbon dioxide, so they are in a different class.

Fortunately, humanity is leaning away from cruel activities such as penning animals, and doing lab experiments. Sporting activities, such as hunting and boxing are also being seen as cruel. Even killing and slaughtering animals by butchers is being seen as disgusting. All of these consciousness changes are being caused by the dawning of the Age of Aquarius. The importance of Life is now more obvious, and important. In the future, all forms of cruelty will be seen as bad behavior.

Soul consciousness takes harm lessons to the extreme. Buddha sat under tree in meditated for 40 days. During that time, he only ate fruit that dropped from the trees of the forest. Wild elephants stayed close by to protect him from tigers. The 40th day is when he became enlightened. Even thoughts and dreams have to be harmless as to not offend god, who exists within you. Thoughts of hatred, anger, and revenge are offensive to god. Daydreams of greatness, Glory, triumph, and power are stupid conceit. There's another all seeing eye of god. It is mother earth, who sees acts of cruelty torture and animals, reptiles, fish and even her plants. That is everything we eat, but fortunately farmers have discovered a way to grow crops in a harmless matter. It is called no till farming. Almost all nutrients are in the top eighth inch of soil. Farmers merely scrape the topsoil into a mound, and plant the seed in the mound. Plants actually grow as well this way as plowing deeply into the soil, which kills earthworms. That's another divine being created by mother earth.

10. Service--- Service is **helping the needs** of

others (**not the wants** of others). Look around and you'll see lots of ways to help others. Forget about feeding, clothing, and housing the poor, for lots of good people are already doing that. Think deeply, and you'll perceive a need that's **not** being met. Then develop your own plan. You may still want to help the poverty stricken, but don't join an organization. March to the beat of your own drum. Start your own organization. Construct a plan that's positive. Protests, boycotts, and destructive techniques are not included, because negative plans will eventually fail. It has to be a constructive plan that ignores the old ways, and focuses on a better way. For example, I have perceived that religion is a mumbo jumbo of beliefs, rituals, dogmas, and Holy Books. The situation is confusing, and very hard for anyone to get a clear view of religion. So my service is to clearly explain how Spiritual Psychology works. Hopefully, that will take the mystery out of religion, and make it easier for seekers to attain enlightenment.

God is the Great Helper who watches and helps. God often helps by encouraging you to help someone. Then at times, God moves others to help you. God also helps by moving you to fulfill your own needs, like getting a job. Don't read lightly over helping others, because this **attitude** has to be in place before enlightenment can happen.

Helping others has healthful benefits. It's especially good at expelling the discomforting feeling of excess energy, which sometimes happens to beginning meditators. Just look around, and you'll see lots of little ways to spontaneously help others. Afterwards, a joyous feeling is experienced, and the excess energy goes away. It's God's reward for helping the Hearts of others.

Religions often describe God as the giver of all good things. That is somewhat misleading, because many parishioners conclude that God is a big sugar daddy. A study found that 49% of all prayers are for money. A better way of praying is to ask for things that can help others.

11. Sharing--- God shares His heart with you. That creates an impulse to share what you have with others.

Many seekers conclude that having nothing is spiritual. So they give everything away, and start walking the path. There's some truth to that, but discarding all of your wealth is not required. What needs to be discarded is your desires, emotions, and imaginings. Wealth is good, because it can be used to help others. It's good for seekers to have some money, because their closeness to God creates wiser ways of sharing it. On the other hand, don't despair if you have no money. There are other valuable things to share, such as your time, energy, knowledge, and attention. What matters is the **sharing attitude**.

Wealth often creates a barrier to higher spirituality. Such as the wealthy are totally focused on their money, possessions, and land. That makes them fearful of losing it to thieves, inflation, and squatters. The soul's attitude is different. The soul is detached from wealth, and sees it as something that can help others. Sometimes, giving it away is the right thing to do. Sometimes, sharing it is the right thing to do, and sometimes being the responsible caretaker is the right thing. The only advice that can be given is,- let the wisdom of your Heart spend it.

12. **Sacrifice**--- Sacrifice is discarding something for the good of others. Sometimes it's necessary for something to be harmed, discarded, or given away, so others may benefit. It could be something extreme, like a mother sacrificing her life to save her child. Being married, and raising a family, often means sacrificing your time, money, and energy to help the little ones. Sacrifice is like giving, except it's a painful giving.

The soul is aware of God's Good, and is willing to sacrifice all to help others. Jesus is an example. He knew that the Messiah had to be crucified, because it was prophesied in the Book of Daniel. Crucifixion is one of the cruelest forms of execution ever invented, and the thought of having to go through it was very disturbing to Jesus; while he was in the Garden of Gethsemane. However, Jesus finally decided to fulfill the scriptures by submitting his life. Think about it. Jesus sacrificed his life so all may understand something about spiritual Love. That was a big contribution to mankind. It changed religions from animal sacrifices, and superstitious beliefs, to teachings about Love.

13. Peace--- Pay attention to this one, because higher spirituality begins when a seeker learns to be peaceful. The emotions and desires have to first become placid. Then the Heart's blessed peacefulness can be felt.

The next level is mental peacefulness. That's

when nary a leaf flutters in the forest of the brain. Meditation is needed for learning how to **see** what the outer mind is doing. Then the imagination becomes still, and you turn into the peaceful detached observer.

Mystics long for a peaceful place to live; and they know that a meditation center is the ideal place. A meditation center's rules and routines are designed to create an atmosphere of peace and solitude. Then everyone becomes like a peaceful island.

14. Serenity--- This is a combination of Love and peace. It can be felt after a deeply peaceful meditation.

15. Patience---This is an expression of the soul's eternal nature. The soul thinks in terms of the eternal now, while humans think in terms of wanting it now. Setbacks, delays, and antics of others are easily tolerated by the soul, for it patiently watches and waits. The patience of an angel is the proper attitude.

16. Detachment--- Disconnecting from the front side.

"I am in this World, but not of it", Jesus said. Pay attention to this one, for it's the gateway. Higher spirituality is often thought of as holy men living in caves, or performing miracles. Some do that, but higher spirituality is really about **detaching** from the outer self, and outer things. Then only the soul remains.

It's common for people to be focused on their front side, or on their imagination, or on something outer. Meditation detaches attention from the body and everything outer. The spotlight will disappear, during deep meditation, and attention then turns inward to the soul and Spirit.

The first task is learning how to detach from the body, pride, desires, and emotions. The second task is learning how to detach from the imagination. When the excited brain becomes still, then a magic moment happens. Consciousness detaches from everything outer, and becomes the detached observer. The outer World is still being seen, but only bare, detached attention is now being paid to anything outer.

People conclude that their land, car, house,

money, etc. belong to them, but in reality, it's the other way around. The old saying of, "That which you possess, will possess you", sums up attachment to possessions. However, attachment to outer things goes wider than just possessions. Such as, people think that they belong to a spouse, family, friends, gang, team, school, community, or nation. All of that changes when a person becomes his soul, for the soul perceives itself as belonging only to divinity.

The Age of Aquarius has made moving from human to soul more difficult. We now have computers and the Internet. So most of the day could be spent looking at interesting things on a computer. We also have a huge variety of books and magazines. So most of the day could be spent looking at paper. Television now has hundreds of different channels, so most of the day could be spent looking at a TV screen. Self entertainment is the problem with those inventions, and detaching from mental pleasure is now harder to do. As a result, meditation will become the New Age Savior. Christ will be arriving to help humanity again, but think about it. Even when Christ does arrive, you'll still have to save yourself. You won't be graduating from school just because a great teacher is visiting

Earth. So learning how to **detach** is the way to escape from Earth's prison of fun and pleasure. You can still own cars, computers, and TVs, but don't let it possess you.

Detachment is a defense mechanism of the soul. It's a harmless way of dealing with bad situations. People often defend themselves by becoming mean, conniving, secretive, talkative, or running away. However, the soul defends itself by detaching. This is a handy tool to have, for I found that detachment works well when faced with angry, hysterical, or depressed people. Think about it. Why feel their emotional sickness? It doesn't help them, and it doesn't help you.

Remaining in a peaceful and detached mood works best, because people will usually compromise their personality to reach a common ground with others. They'll control their emotions when around someone that's peaceful and detached. However, some can't see outside of their own drama, but they can be easily disarmed by saying "You look upset", or "You're in a bad mood". That makes an emotionally trapped person stop and think about what they are doing.

17.   Observer--- The watcher, witness, or onlooker.

All seekers have a master that occasionally checks up on them. When a seeker becomes the detached observer, then he's a junior member of the Great White Brotherhood. His master can then send a message.

When the outer mind becomes still, then consciousness becomes a detached observer. What may be noticed is that the eyes are now more clearly looking at the floor, instead of gazing.

Many think that mystical practices and Yoga postures will make them spiritual, but that's not true. They are still focused on their front side feelings. What seekers need to do is meditate. Then consciousness can detach from the emotional chest, and enter the detached Heart. That's when the magical world of peacefulness is entered. The next magical world happens when attention stops spotlighting the frontal cortex. Then the imagination and verbal intellect stops working. After that, consciousness will move a little to the rear, and enter the intuitive Mind. That's when a seeker becomes the detached observer. His mind is like a light bulb again. He's only observing, but a detached observer isn't observing in a strong or intense manner. He is paying only bare attention to what's out there. A feeling of being "in this World, but not of it", can then be noticed.

The observer may watch the movements of his outer self, after a meditation ends. Such as, seeing the hand slowly reaching out to pick up a cup of tea, and watching the hand slowly move the cup up to the lips. There's a feeling of drinking the tea, and noticing the taste. Talking is more astounding, in that someone up front seems to be doing the talking, and the words are echoing back to where you're at. This is called mindfulness, or full of Mind.

It's hard for a detached observer to function in the human world. The ego has disappeared, and relating with common folks is now more difficult. That means a soul personality has to be created. The soul has to learn how much detachment can be allowed in this or that situation. The soul also has to learn how to use the Heart's Love and wisdom for relating with others. Then it's possible to remain in contact with the soul at all times.

The observer has a clear and natural way of seeing. Desires, emotions, and imagination energy are not driving the observer to think. It merely sees everything as it is, and watches movement. It could be said that the observer is one step away from the pure mind of god's intuition, which seeks the whole thing, or big picture. The observer can be entered fairly easy. Relax the face and let the eyes gaze. Lower the eyelids down to where the lower part of the room is seen, and start meditating. If a dream interrupts the meditation, then realize that your desire character was getting bored, and was wanting some fun or pleasure by creating some money, power, superiority, greatness, and heroic glory, or planning on building a futuristic utopia. Shut it down, when seen, and return back to being only the peaceful observer.

18. Centered--- A deeply centered feeling happens, when reaching the soul. It's something like the end of a play where the curtains close, and the actor becomes his self again. In this case, centeredness feels like becoming the natural self again.

The Heart is the center of your being, and a Loving centeredness is felt when consciousness moves away from the emotional side to reside in the radiant Heart. The first time it happens will always be remembered.

A **mentally** centered feeling also happens when the imagination is dismissed, and you become a detached observer.

19. Living in Truth--- Probationers realize the value of ending their lies, scams, and excuses. Then they can live in truth. The reward is a feeling of relief, because lying is stressful.

A higher level is when seekers realize that there's a difference between thinking and reality. Desires, pride, and emotions drive the imagination to create thoughts. But the imagined thoughts are unreal.

A seeker's goal is to become truth. Jesus expressed it when he said, "I am the way, the truth, and the light". However, an interesting thing happened when Pilate asked him, "What is truth"? Jesus remained silent. Can you imagine that? One of mankind's most spiritually intelligent was stumped by that question. Unfortunately, neither can I give a good answer. About the only thing known about truth is that it will remain true for thousands of years. So truth will have to be defined as - that which is. Another definition would be,- what is, is, and what isn't, isn't. The closest word to truth is **obvious**.

An interesting thing is that God creates what will be happening in the future. Even thousands of years into the future. That means we are living in God's dream. So if this is God's dream, then what kind of truth is that?

20. Reality ---Shakespeare said, "The whole world is a stage, and we are the actors." What he didn't say is everyone has three divine entities watching us act. It has been going on day and night since we were born. One entity is the guardian angel. Another is the all seeing eye of mother earth. The third is god himself, he is within, watching our every thought, dream, and emotion. It is amazing to think that we have never had a moment of privacy during our entire lives.

12. THE OUTER SELF

EMOTIONS -- The words emotions and feelings will be interchangeable in this book.

A radiant ball of Love exists within the chest of everyone. This energy interacts with nerves on the chest to create rosy, affectionate, and cheery feelings. Unfortunately, suffering feelings also exist on the chest. Your Hell on Earth is created by the feelings of anger, shame, sadness, and fear. Below are some suggestions on how to dissolve the 4 suffering emotions. You may know of other ways. If so, then spread the word.

CONTROLLING FEAR panic, terror, fright, anxiety, dread, and worry

All fears are in the future.

But the future hasn't yet happened.

Therefore, fear is unreal.

One way is to get rid of fear is to relax. Then it's possible to see that you were imagining a future tragedy. Fear will disappear when acknowledging that it was only imagined.

Some find worry to be useful. They are convinced that worrying about all possible outcomes prepares them for future calamities. A lot of needless suffering is thereby created, because seldom does anything bad happen. One way to get rid of worry is to become tired of it. Conclude that you don't want to think about that nagging worry. Accept whatever will be the outcome. Be courageous, and think,- what will be will be, and let me deal with it when it happens. There's an old adage that says. "A brave man dies once, while a coward dies a thousand times".

Fear itself is able to create bad situations, such as, becoming scared when a dog barks at you. Dogs attack when seeing cowardice. So if an attack does occur, then the injury was caused by fear.

CONTROLLING GUILT shame, disgrace, regret

The soul becomes disappointed, whenever you harm someone. That's the origin of guilt. A good way to eliminate guilt is to admit that you messed up, and then repay the harmed person. But if repayment is not possible, then visualize a better way of doing it.

Mistakes are good, because we are here on Earth to learn how **not** to do things. Each mistake reveals a roughness that needs to be polished. Eventually, you'll become a perfect gem. Hopefully, it will be this lifetime.

The detached soul has a big task to perform. The soul has to humble the arrogant outer self in order to get control over it. That's a tough job when considering that the soul's only tools are sickness, guilt, and fear of death. So everyone has to experience many episodes of pain and guilt before learning the right way to live.

Guilt sometimes flashes forth during meditation. Stupid things said, or done, are recalled as the mind becomes clearer. This is a self cleaning process that sometimes happens when getting close to the Pure Self. The best way to deal with old and forgotten memories is to admit that you made a stupid mistake. Then visualize a better way of doing it.

CONTROLLING SADNESS and DEPRESSION

Everyone is a sensitive being that feels sad when losing something valuable, like a car, house, or beloved friend. Fortunately, there are lots of ways to get past sadness. One way is to remain in pleasurable state. Drugs and alcohol work well, but everyone knows that is not a good answer. Another way is to believe in better days to come, like when winning a lottery. Hardening the heart also works, but nobody likes a hard hearted person. Staying busy by working long hours, or by watching movie after movie, takes the mind off sadness. However, the best solution is to understand the problem by talking to a good listener. That can stop the rain in minutes.

The good times with loved ones creates fondness, but sadness happens when the beloved friend is lost. Fortunately, time erases bad memories, and heals the emotional wounds. Take lots of naps, for sleep is good memory eraser. Also, think about resignation. If the beloved friend can never return, then you'll have to walk away from the memory of him or her.

I worked with a person that cried a lot about trivial problems, which were mostly caused by her own negligence. I asked if she would like to eliminate the sadness. Her reply was "Oh no. Sadness is natural and normal". Obviously, there's something about sadness that she liked. That is inconceivable, but it's an example of how people become attached to suffering feelings.

Depression is like sadness, but a bit different. Some depression is due to chemical problems, like toxins, alcohol, and drugs. Some is due to the brain decaying during old age. Some depression is caused by low hormone levels. Some is due to being imprisoned by poverty, or a dominating spouse. A boring job also takes its toll. A good solution is to talk with a good listener, for it's possible to arrive at an obvious solution within minutes. That's better than "holding it in, and growing a tumor", as Woody Allen once said. However, talking to a friend isn't always the best solution, because friends usually give advice. The best listeners are psychologists. Their technique is to keep asking questions until you clearly see the problem. Then the psychologist will ask, "So what are you going to do about it"? It's your problem, and you're the best one to perceive what can or cannot work. Psychologists are expensive, but it's better than spending your money on alcohol, or continuing to live with daily suffering.

"Burn out" with your job or spouse creates depression. A change is needed, such as quitting, or taking a long vacation. Resolving the problem through a mediator also works. Burn out is an emotional disease that needs to be recognized, because it makes your miserable situation go on and on.

Society pressures us to self stimulate. We learned at an early age how to intensify desire, so as to become quicker at sports or video games. Also, many choose to become the fastest talker, so as to charm, or overpower others. Some even go to the extreme by making their mind move at a thousand miles per hour. They talk fast, and many ideas appear in their head. That makes them think that they are superior to the slower thinking public. The speed problem needs to be recognized, because high mental speed fatigues the brain. Depression and mental breakdowns can then occur.

Increasing your spiritual brightness works well for getting rid of a dark depression. Helping others works best, such as, giving some money to a lowly beggar. That makes the Heart glow brighter, and the heaviness disappears. Also, go to church, and be around joyous parishioners. Being joyous is a good way to climb out of a deep, dark depression.

CONTROLLING ANGER hate, rage, vengeance, hostility, negativity, and irritation

There's no good use for anger. It has to be eliminated. Feeling the tingling nerves is a good way to get rid of anger, because that's a bad feeling. Then notice that you don't like that feeling, and the anger disappears.

A lot of irritation is created by sickness, fatigue, hunger, menstrual periods, etc. Unfortunately, many think that expressing their irritation is the best way to get rid of it. They think,- "rag on someone. Get it out, and you'll feel better". It works, but expressing irritation is a dumb way to get relief, because it harms friendships. The best way is to acknowledge that you are sick, and then get some sleep.

Someone harming you creates anger. You can carry the pain of being unjustly hurt for the rest of your life, but seekers are smarter than that. They can see the advantage of forgiving. Try praying for the one that hurt you. That is hard to do. But why let someone's stupid act burn you forever? After feeling forgiveness, then keep away from the harmful one. Chances are, if he was dumb enough to hurt you once, then he'll do it again. It's best to remain clear of anger, because it can turn on you. Such as accidents happen during an angry mood, or shortly after the anger has ended. So it's best to conclude that all forms of anger have to be eliminated.

Negativity is one way to measure a person's spiritual level. Angry people often curse, and are seldom in a good mood. Cruel people are worse, for they find anger to be useful. According to the master Djwhal Khul, "insanity will be their lot in the next lifetime". This is not a punishment, because God doesn't think that way. Insanity is God's way of busting a person's cruelty habit.

The here and now is where you want to be. Many spend their entire day worrying about the future. Others are immersed in memories of a depressing loss, or are feeling guilty about a past deed, or feeling angry about being unjustly hurt. All of these suffering feelings are about the past or future. The cure is to relax, and see what your mind is doing. Then it's easy to return to the here and now. That's when the World becomes a happy place again.

DESIRE want, wish, crave, lust, hope, yearn, covet, and aspire

A newborn baby notices that a full belly creates a warm, and pleasurable feeling. As a result, the baby becomes attentive to his tummy. That is the origin of the desire self, which is a sucker for fun and good feelings.

Desire is like a friend and teacher during childhood, but needs to be studied and controled. A good mother, or teacher is needed up to the age of 21. After that, painful lessons are needed for learning how not to do things. The age of 30 is when a person's soul begins to emerge, and a conflict with desire also begins to emerge.

Desire also loves stories. Fictional stories found in books, magazines, and movies. This conflicts with the soul, which lives in truth. Desire loves money and the power that money gives to the wealthy. Desire loves to daydream, especially the greatness and glory dreams of pride. Desire loves parties, dancing, and sex. It should be apparent that higher spirituality means giving up all that is fun and pleasurable. It sounds bad, but old age will make you give it up, for pleasure and pain are like two sides of a coin. When the body starts hurting, and the mind becomes crazy, or feeble, then it's time to change. The funster has to be evicted, and start living a pleasant life.

The blending of desire with God's Will produces an energy known as will power. This is a driving energy that makes the muscles strain harder, but willful determination has a dark side. It creates selfishness and self centeredness. Strong will power also creates fanaticism, which is a hard headedness that ignores what others are saying, so as to remain focused on only their point of view. So will power should only be used for making the muscles strain harder.

Under the frontal lobes of the brain is the mental control center. It's where the radiant light of Mind focuses into a beam of light, or searchlight. Desire swings the searchlight up, down, and anywhere around to focus on feelings, imaginings, muscles, and cravings. When it's focused on the frontal cortex, then the wheels of mind start spinning. All you have to do is **want** to see a memory, and it appears. All you have to do is **want** to see a possibility, and it appears. All you have to do is **want** to imagine something, and a picture appears.

All of your thoughts appear to be correct, but the thoughts were slanted by thinking what you **want** to think. So how real is that?

Mix desire with emotions, and a funster is created. The funster likes to have fun, pleasure, pride, greatness, and self goodness. On the other side of the coin is the painster. The painster slants its thinking towards anger, fear, death, and destruction. So mixing desire with emotions creates a lot of weird thinking.

Another weird thinking problem happens when desire mixes with belief. Some will deliberately **believe** that their thoughts and dreams are true, because they **want** it to be true. That's how delusions are created. Delusions are false beliefs that are a little crazy.

Desire is a hard one to control, for it's seldom noticed . A good way to control desire is to stop focusing on wants, and start thinking in terms of needs. Also, recognize any yearning, wishing, hoping, and craving that crosses the mind. That's important, because awareness of a spontaneous desire will make it disappear. Moving less also helps, as desire drives the muscles. Another tip is to eat less, for the belly is desire's energy center. Fasting works better, because the desire self is knocked down to nearly nothing after three days of fasting.

Relaxation, self awareness, and detachment makes desire disappear. Two other anti-desire tools are silence and seclusion. A good way to get some seclusion is to camp at a remote location. It takes courage to be out there by yourself, but there's no need to worry. The animals are more scared of you, than you are of them. Seldom does any threat arise, but if it does, then your soul will know what to do.

Aspiration is desiring to be better than what you are. Such as children aspire to be grown up, while adults aspire to be wealthy and great. There's also a noble form of desire called spiritual aspiration. That happens when feeling the soul's radiant Love, and then yearning to become more spiritual. Mystics aspire to become the peaceful soul, while contemplators aspire to become enlightened. But it doesn't end at enlightenment, because adepts and masters also aspire to become more spiritual.

The desire self mixes with pride and emotions to create the ego, which is called I, me, myself. Everyone is convinced that their ego's proud feelings, and intellects are real, because that's all they know about their self. However, everything changes, when discovering the inner self's Love.

Then a person seeks to become their inner self. They intuitively know that fun, pleasure, and desire have to end. That's when the desire self starts to slowly die. The end is called "the second death". Pride, desire, and self entertainment has died. Then the soul is the driver of everything said, thought, and done.

Almost everyone has a 12 year old child within. Actually it is three children. One is a desire kid who loves to have fun. This funster is mostly focused on playing games, so as to be triumphant. The second inner child is pride. This as a close brother to the funster, in that pride is really a self image child, who loves superiority, greatness, and heroic glory. War games are its favorite. The third inner child is emotions. Pleasurable feelings are its favorite, although the emotional child is also burdened with four painful feelings. There is a very troublesome child, but women seem to love the emotions. Its biggest problem is with addiction to anything with pleasurable feelings like drugs, alcohol, and sex. Desire plays a big part with addictions, so desire and emotions are related. There's not much hope that a normal person will be able to control their talker with self awareness and the two above suggestions. It will take a strong willed person to control their desire, imagination, and talker complex which is most of the ego.

The best way to achieve mental control over the ego is to surrender. Move control out of the high and mighty forehead, and move consciousness down to the chest's humble heart. You will become a peaceful and humble person that thinks with the intuitive mind and speaks with wisdom. That is a good choice. The tense and exhausting rat race has ended, and god is helping with everyday chores. What you lose is desire's fun, ambition, superiority, plus cravings for money power, and sex. But the peacefulness, love, and joy makes a better lifestyle. And that's worth living.

Desire drives the whole body. It drives everything we say, think, and do, so it could be said that humans are desire beings. Desire drives the muscles to move. It also drives the tongue, jaw, and lips to move. Thus speech is thereby created. Sounds vibrate the roof of the mouth, which acts like a drum to a blob of brain just above the roof. That blob is your verbal intellect. Desire sends verbal sound signals up to the foreheads imagination where speech recognition is produced. In addition, words heard in the ears are compared with mouth sounds, language is thus produced in children. At some point in a person's life, he learns how to use the verbal blob and imagination combo to think, plan, and invent. Thus the verbal intellect is born.

A person that becomes a soul notices how society is filled with childish adults, ambitious people, and lots of half insane people. The soul centered ones realize they are not of this world, and are centered on the back side and focus their attention between the shoulder blades. To remain there, self awareness must see every desire and thought that floats by, and make it disappear. He has to be totally finished with desire, or the ego funster will reappear. He is allowed to miss a few times, and have ego's dreaming appear, but too much of that he'll be a human again. So remain vigilant to totally eliminate desire.

PRIDE Self admiration

A deep noble feeling can be sensed after a meditation ends. The noble feeling originates from God's Goodness, which is located at the tailbone. Unfortunately, most of humanity prefers to transform their divine feeling of

God's Good into the proud feelings of honor, majesty, greatness, and self goodness. That spurs them on to compete for wealth and superiority.

Pride creates lots of suffering. It makes us do stupid things, like being daring, or working hard. The irony of working hard is we do it to achieve honors and wealth, but we can't express it, because nobody likes a braggart.

The energy of God's Goodness flows up the spine of a soul man, and then down the front side. Humans are different, in that their Goodness energy flows up the front side, and connects with the emotions. Then it changes into pride and superiority. From there, pride moves up to the head, and changes into thoughts of greatness and glory. The relaxation practice of watching the sinking feeling of the outgoing breath works well for pushing pride back down. Pride can also be pushed down by feeling the chest sink. That happens naturally when being defeated.

What's been said about pride seems to

paint a negative picture, but it does have a good aspect. Many keep a tight reign on their actions, so as to maintain a good reputation. So pride can be a helpful tool for both the individual and society.

SELF IMAGE   The imagined self.

The ego is referred to as I, me, myself. It's a combination of pride, desires, and emotions. The ego enjoys imagining itself as being higher, greater, smarter, and wealthier than others. Those traits are bundled into an imagined self called **self image**. The more possessions and traits in the bundle, the greater the self image.

The age of 2, is when the little funsters begin to notice that they are being called a name, like John. Then a concept is created that they are John. Awareness of abilities are added like I can walk, and I can talk. A sense of possession is included, like this is my mother, and this is my toy. A rating of one's height, age, cuteness, strength, and smartness is included. Copying others is also added. The parents are the first ones copied, and the villager's personalities are next. If men of the village have strong and brave personalities, then boys will copy those. Or if the men have generous, loving personalities, then boys will copy those.

The growth of self image continues as should-bes and shouldn't- bes are added. Young men have problems with honor, superiority, and how to act around girls. Many solve those problems by concluding that they should be well dressed, witty, strong, brave, sophisticated, smooth talking, etc. On the other side, they shouldn't be wimpy, cowardly, stupid, sloppy, etc. The addition of should-bes and shouldn't-bes adds stress to the psyche, because it's a lie, and lying is stressful.

Young people also have the problem of thinking that an actor is needed for relating with others. Then their life becomes one act after another, and their style of acting becomes the personality. That adds color to the self image, but it's phony.

It's interesting how people identify with money and clothes. If a person has a big stash of money, then they say it's mine, all mine. I'm rich. I'm not a peasant anymore. The same thing happens with clothes. If a person dons blue jeans and a T shirt, then they're an ordinary person. If they put on a suit, then they're a high class business man, or executive. On the other hand, when everyone removes their clothes, like at a naked swimming party, then everyone becomes equal. Somehow, money and clothes make the self image go way up, or way down.

Self-image has no reality to it. A snapshot of your physical self shows how the self now looks. But the self looked a lot different during childhood, and it looks different during old age, when the hair is gray, and the face is wrinkled. So looking at the body is not a good way to describe yourself. Unfortunately, there's nothing lasting about the outer self. What you have is a snapshot of right now, and that continues to change.

13. ELIMINATING ADDICTIONS

Pleasure turns your prop. It's the biggest reason why people do the things they do. If pleasure is experienced, then you'll yearn for more. Therein lies the addiction problem.

Probationers are struggling with their addictions to physical pleasures. Mystics are struggling with their addiction to emotional pleasures. And contemplators are struggling with their mental pleasures. That's a simple way of describing the path, however, most seekers are struggling with pleasure on all 3 levels.

Everyone thinks of using will power to eliminate an addiction, but will power is hardened desire. That means using desire to eliminate desire. It works, but hard headed will power eventually softens. A person then thinks that it's ok to have another cigarette. But the addiction returns with the first puff, and a person is back to buying cigarettes again.

Monotony is another way to eliminate an addiction, because we always tire of the same old thing. An example would be with smoking marijuana. That can be a hard habit to quit, because there's very little pain on the negative side, and lots of pleasure on the positive side. One way to kick the habit is to smoke it every day. Keep on doing it for years, and you'll eventually become tired of the same old high. Then it's time to quit. Unfortunately, the monotony technique doesn't work well with alcohol and tobacco. Those addictions require awareness and analysis. A positive and negative list works well for those substances.

Addiction is usually thought of as wanting alcohol, drugs, or tobacco, but addiction is really a **craving for another rosy feeling on the chest**. What's needed is a cool, detached look at the addiction, and meditating is the easy way to do it. Make a positive and negative list during the morning meditation. That produces a clear picture of the problem, and then you'll know what to do.

The ability to inhibit thoughts is vital for seekers to remain on the path. Inhibition is being able to curb cravings and addictions. The problem is certain substances like tobacco, alcohol, hard drugs, and marijuana make the brain release dopamine, which produces a pleasurable feeling. What makes the dopamine pleasure bad is the 12 year old boy and funster who wants to get higher. His ego, which is a combination of self image, pride, and desire, wants more and more of that pleasurable stuff. Fortunately there's an ego controller inside your head. It is inhibition, the ability to say no more to fun and pleasure. Tobacco is the third most addictive substance behind heroin and cocaine. Scientists have concluded that it creates at least 20 types of cancer. Combine alcohol with tobacco and it becomes a killer. I had two aunts, a sister, and a wife who combined alcohol with tobacco daily, and all four died of different forms of cancer. Heroin and cocaine are the most addictive substances, and the hardest ones to kick. What's sad about hard drugs is they drive the ego to overdose. Another bad point is the addictive craving drives the ego to steal and commit armed robbery. Marijuana is considered to be a harmless drug but destroys a seeker's spirituality by distracting the ability to remain focused on a subject, like relaxing or a mantra. Marijuana feels like, and seems to be spiritual, because it connects a user with his soul and energies. Unfortunately the high makes a user feel like a fun loving child again. The ability to remain focused on a single subject is lost, and daydreaming begins. That's when even the most brightly spiritual can fall from grace. Then they have to rebuild their ability to hold their minds still or steady. The wandering ego starts playing with the verbal intellect, by creating stories that are turned into daydreaming brain movies. Those movies are also addictive.

Drugs make a person feel spiritual for about 10 or 15 minutes. Marijuana is the best one for getting a spiritual high. The mind becomes calm and things are clear seeing new things that were never noticed before. The body is energized and feelings of divine love, and love is seen everywhere. However, this glimpse of a higher spirituality lasts for all of 5 minutes. Then the party spirit wipes it away off to laughter and an hour of fun fun fun. Two thirds humanity remain at a 12 year old mentality. It could be said that a person goes from 12 back to a nine year old on marijuana. That is not spiritual progress when smoking marijuana. So how can a person quickly become highly spiritual? The first answer is to discard fun and pleasure, and the 12 year old child disappears. The second answer is to a meditate lot, and occasionally fast, so as to have a clear mind and receive intuitive answers to questions. And a three day fast during full Moon time, or when the Moon is in Taurus works good. Also meditate upon awakening and before going to bed every day.

14. SEX

There's a legend that millions of years ago, we were angels on Planet Earth. Some of the angels became fascinated with animals having sex, and entered the bodies of animals so as to enjoy the pleasure of sex. Then it became clear that Earth angels had a weakness. So bodies were created for the errant angels. That is said to be the origin of humanity. This is an interesting legend, but it may not be true.

It's best to start by saying that nobody has all the answers on sex, and neither do I. This is a really tough subject, because the genitals keep building up energy. Then interest in playing with someone else's body takes center stage. Try to shake off the craving, and it keeps on returning.

We become attracted to others during childhood, and having a loving spouse appears to be the ultimate achievement. Boys gain the warm affectionate nature of their mother, while girls gain the protective, giving nature of their father. Things usually go well during the first year of marriage when hot sexual love keeps the couple in a drugged state. However, the bubble bursts when a woman realizes that her dream of having a big house, family, and security won't be happening. Or a man's dream of having a warm loving mother bursts when his wife becomes mean, during her menstrual cycle. So the question becomes, why don't schools teach classes on marital problems? Classes are given on how the sex organs work, but nothing is said about relationship problems. A lot of misery, and crying the blues, could be avoided if teens knew how the marriage dance really works.

The paradox of sex is, abstaining from it is spiritual, yet, experiencing sex is also spiritual. The emotions become placid after a climax, and only the radiant soul remains. If more sexual experiences happen, then the Hearts connect, and the couple falls in love. The feeling of devotion and sacrifice can get to be so overwhelming that a man is willing to "sleep out in the rain for his lover". That quote, from a song, sounds excessive, but logic cancels out when a man is in love. The love connection can become so strong that a couple will dance soul to soul for the rest of their lives. That's a good thing, because devotion, sacrifice, and serving a family creates a good atmosphere for spiritual growth.

Sex produces a feeling of oneness, and the couple is automatically married in Spirit. Then the couple will want to express their deep love for each other by having a marriage ceremony. That's when they proclaim their love to God and everyone. It's a ceremony where their Heart is being given to their beloved mate. However, giving your Heart away is dangerous. Most people remain a 13 year old throughout their entire life, and trusting your Heart to a big kid is risky. They can easily stab you in the Heart, or break your Heart. Nobody knows whether their Heart will be used, abused, or tenderly prized by a potential sex mate. So if you see any meanness in a potential mate, then run away. That's because marriages usually degenerate into one being dominant, and the other being a wimp. Needless to say, the harmless seeker becomes the wimp. So seekers should marry only seekers. Let the mean ones walk alone, or find a mate that's equally nasty.

It appears as though the answer is to marry someone that's highly spiritual, because a lot of childish tantrums, criticism, and arguments are eliminated. Unfortunately, most of the highly spiritual male seekers will have to remain single, because there's usually two men for each woman on the higher path,

Most do choose to be single, but that creates problems. The soul glows brighter for mystics, and the extra loving energy increases their sexual appetite. If a seeker engages in sex, then he encounters the problem of addiction, because sex is very addictive. All it takes is doing it once. The next day, he'll recall how much fun it was, and will want to do it again. Then he'll be doing it again and again until they are married in Spirit. Unfortunately, everything becomes old, and it's easy to lose sight of a mate's soul. A divorce in Spirit then happens, and the loser will be crying the blues. It's usually the seeker.

A romantic break up is worse than drugs, in that the pain can last for 6 months. It can get to be so bad that some will kill themselves, or their mate, or both, during the withdrawal. Coming down off drugs is easier, because a drug withdrawal usually lasts about four days, and nobody kills their self for not having drugs.

Intimate love is so sweet that just one encounter can trap you in a bad marriage for the rest of your life. So causal sex is not an answer. Neither is hiring a prostitute, because it's also possible to become addicted to a prostitute. The bottom line is, be very careful about choosing a sex partner.

Choosing homosexuality is **not** an answer, because it's a perversion of your natural gender. To put it simply, what you have between your legs is for making babies. Homosexual sex is lots of fun, but it leads to imagining yourself as being of a different sex. It also leads to lots of suffering, because gay boys usually have more relationships, and cry the blues more often, than heterosexuals. However, some are born homosexual, like little boys that prefer playing with dolls and girls. For them, homosexuality is natural, and there should be no guilt. On the other hand, most of the homosexuals "came out of the closet". They tried it. They liked it, and now imagine themselves as being of both sexes. That's wrong, because men have a natural instinct to penetrate, and give of themselves. Women have a natural instinct to give of themselves by receiving. Imagining yourself as being something different is phony. So relieving pressure through homosexual acts is not an answer.

The sexual flame usually ignites in the head. All it takes to awaken sexual desire in the brain is a picture, thought, hint, or being touched in a sensitive area. The desire for sex awakens, and getting rid of it is harder than getting rid of a pesky fly at mealtime. A warm affectionate feeling then blossoms on the chest, and goes down to the crotch. The craving gets hotter, and a climax is urgently needed. One way to control sexual desire is to catch it early. Don't be laying down. Get up and walk around. Try switching attention to another subject, like reading, designing, or watching TV.

The best way to eliminate a sexual feeling is to focus on the spiritual Heart. Focusing on the Heart swings attention away from the emotions, and to a different World. Then focus on the 3rd eye, because the 3rd eye also exists in a different World. The combination of Heart and 3rd eye makes it easy to turn attention away from sexual imaginings. This method works well for seekers, because they are already in battle between the desire self and Pure Self.

Another way to make the urge stop, besides taking a cold shower, is to change attention from your front side to the upper back side, spine, and heart chakra. It will take a few minutes for the pesky urge to disappear. Then change the subject by reading, watching TV, or talking to someone.

Another solution is to remain peacefully centered in the soul. Then sexual thoughts seldom appear. But if an impulse does occur, then swat it away by saying to yourself, that's not what I want. Being a noble prude works quite well.

The hardest time to control sexual feelings is when laying in bed at night. The best way to deal with this problem is to be creative. Design or plan something, for about 10 minutes. Then the desire self will have forgotten about pleasure. However, if a tinge of sexual disappointment is felt, then go back to creating, because a little ember of desire can make the emotions flame up again. Keep on creating until you are completely free of sexual craving.

What you eat can make a difference. Eat a lot of food, and attention focuses on a pleasant feeling belly. The crotch is just below, and the pleasant energy can drift down to the genitals. Also, what you eat makes a difference. Eat some sweets, and the cheery feeling is a reminder of the sweetness of sex. Drink some wine, and a jolly feeling happens. Then the inhibitions dissolve, and who cares anymore? Lets do it. A good way to eliminate these problems is to avoid alcohol, hot sauce, meat, and sweets. Eat only when hungry, and then eat a small meal.

Divorce is usually wrong. On the other hand, divorce is right for the spiritually minded man that's over 50, and his children are over 18. Let the woman have everything, and hit the spiritual trail.

Making the break is tough, because an oath has to be broken. But the good thing about divorce is it frees you from the "tender trap". The spiritual trail usually ends in poverty, but that's a blissful escape from the toughest addiction of all, which is sex.

I don't like to advocate divorce, because it's hard on everyone. However, it's not much of problem if the children are over 18, because they are old enough to live on their own. If the children are under the age of 10, then they are better off living with their mother. If they are over 10, then it's different story. Studies have shown that children, over the age of 10 will mature more naturally when living with a parent of the same gender.

It's best for seekers to consider being asexual, which means abstaining. Celibacy is a bit different, in that celibacy is usually done for purity and devotional reasons. The urge to be asexual often happens when catching a wider view on the pain of sexual imprisonment. Then it becomes obvious that the folly of sex has to end.

Total abstinence is **not** a good practice, because the sex organs are like the bladder. Both have to be occasionally drained. Going more than 90 days without a climax makes the genitals very sensitive, and the decrease in sex hormones can create health problems. Sometimes the body will solve the problem by having a wet dream at night, but if that doesn't happen, then masturbation will have to be the answer.

Is that the final answer? I do not know. What I have learned is that sex is a land where wise men fear to tread.

15. WEALTH

Money is good. It's needed to exist, and learn lessons in life. Some people hold large amounts of wealth, because being rich is part of God's plan. For many others, wealth is a test to see how riches will affect them. Flunking the test means that the next lifetime will be spent in humbling poverty. That would not be a punishment, but a learning situation. Think about it. If you were God, how would you correct a person's greedy, hoarding, and elitist attitudes? The answer is to take him to the extremes. That builds self awareness.

Lots of money doesn't mean that the owner gets a wider view on life. In fact, just the opposite usually happens. Most of the wealthy think they are part of the elite, and above those lower class peasants. Also, many of the wealthy can't see what's wrong with taxing the poor, or giving them only minimum wages.

A good aspect of poverty is that it keeps seekers on the path. One example is a psychic reading done by Edgar Cayce. Edgar wondered why he could never make lots of money off his super psychic abilities, so he did a psychic reading on the question. The answer came back, "The entity is remaining poor, because if wealthy, he would spend all of his money on women".

Some seekers conclude that they can become highly spiritual by giving all their wealth to a guru. What they don't know is that they are giving away the wrong things. Higher spirituality is an attitude. The outer self's pride, desires, emotions, and imaginings are the things to be given away. The best policy is to retain some of the wealth and possessions, but keep it to a minimum. Also, stop thinking in terms of wants, and start thinking in terms of needs. Then, you don't have to earn as much money. It's a spend less, work less, philosophy.

Poverty is a prison with no walls, but poverty is also a classroom where many good things are learned. I went through years of extreme poverty. There were times when I didn't know how I would survive, but food and shelter always appeared. Apparently, there wasn't much to worry about, because the spiritual side was always watching and helping. I wasn't alone either, for the poor huddle together and help each other. It turns out that poverty is an invisible brotherhood that nobody knows about, until they're also broke and homeless.

Everyone thinks that being wealthy will make their life more pleasant, but just the opposite usually happens. A lot of time, effort, and worrying has to be spent trying to safeguard the treasure from inflation, thieves, fire, rust, rot, termites, etc. So freedom from insecurity doesn't happen by being rich. What everyone needs to realize is that all land and money belong to God. We can only be caretakers of God's wealth. However, it's good for seekers to have some wealth, because it can be spent helping others.

16. BREATH FOLLOWING

Focusing on the breath works best when feeling sick, tired, or tense, because the deep peacefulness recharges the body in a different way than sleep. It feels like the body has been infused with a new kind of energy.

If you have a job that's highly mental, attentive, busy, or quick reacting, then an after work meditation is needed. Thirty minutes of doing a mantra, or watching the slow breath, works well for unwinding, and becoming normal again.

Every meditation should be started by a breath following practice, because (A), it's the best way to get centered in the Heart, and (B), the Heart's peacefulness needs to be in place before going on to a mental practice. If the emotions are **not** peaceful, then the imagination will continue to generate lots of thoughts and stories.

Breath following is focusing on the outgoing breath. The incoming breath is stimulating, whereas the outgoing breath is relaxing. The longer the outgoing breath is focused upon, the slower it becomes. Keep on meditating, and the breath can become so slow that it will even stop. Some Yogis have put on demonstrations where they stop breathing for as long as 3 weeks. How they do it is unknown, but it works well for wowing others.

Another astounding thing happens when peacefulness reaches a profound level that's impossible to describe. That's because the words needed to describe it haven't been invented.

The most popular practice is to feel the outgoing breath touching the ends of the nostrils. The ida and pingala nerves start at the ends of the nostrils, and go down the spine to the end. Then the nerves go back up the spine to the Mind center. That makes the Mind center light up, and light flows through the 3rd eye tunnel to the 3rd eye. That makes its chakra light up.

A more mental version of breath following is to focus on the breath going out, and then dissipating.

Start a breath following meditation by leaning way forward, and feeling the backside muscles stretch. Then arch the whole spine forward while sitting up. Remain focused on the upper back side and spine, so as to keep attention away from the front side's desires and emotions. Next, sound the HUM, or MM, with each outgoing breath. Do that for a minute or two, and then start focusing on the feeling of the outgoing breath touching the ends of the nostrils. Also observe the sinking feeling of the outgoing breath, for that helps to move consciousness inward to the Heart. Continue focusing on the outgoing breath touching the nostrils, and eventually, the detached observer will be reached. The Mind of your soul will doing the observing.

If a dream interrupts, then go back to the Heart, and start over again. Doing the HU or UU helps to clear away dream dust. Then return to watching the slow breath touching the nostrils.

Breath following is the meditation of deep peacefulness, but peacefulness is hard to maintain in our fast paced society. Any sound or movement will disturb the peace. I tried for years to find a peaceful lifestyle outside of the monastery, but finally gave up. It turns out that we have to be mental, as well as peaceful, in the Aquarian Age. So it's best to also learn how to contemplate. That's explained in chapters 21 and 23.

Sometimes the mind refuses to calm down due to sore muscles or body irritants. Breath counting and mantras are also used, but all is not lost. Try doing the simplest kind of Breath following. Which is only watching the outgoing breath. This practice produces a deep peacefulness.

MIND

17. MASS MIND - herd mentality

There's an old saying that "a newborn lamb doesn't fear the lion". The mind of a little lamb is completely blank. It learns by watching its mother, and by following along with what others in the herd are doing. After becoming mature, the lamb will continue to follow along with what the herd is doing. Nary an original thought will ever appear in his head. This is mass mind, or herd mentality.

Writers, orators, politicians, and television sway the minds of the masses. Then the masses respond by waving flags, cheering, and joining the army. The masses also follow fads in clothing, haircuts, dance, slang, art, decorating, etc. Most are convinced that following along with what's popular is the way to go. They think that the perfect lifestyle is to be rich, powerful, married, and have lots of possessions.

The folly of mass thought may be seen, when a psychedelic drug is taken. That's when some will drop out, and start marching to the beat of their own drum. They become the "black sheep of the family", but dropouts enjoy a freedom that the masses don't know about. They have discovered that it's nicer to be poor and single, than to be another tired rat in the rat race.

18. COMMON SENSE

Common sense is using your senses to act or react. It's like seeing a car coming straight at you, and you automatically jump out of the way. Or putting on more clothes when feeling cold. Or not eating food that tastes rotten. Common sense knows by seeing, hearing smelling, tasting, and feeling.

19. EMOTIONAL MIND

The emotions work in a way that can't be defined as mental, because emotions are unable to put 2 plus 2 together. However, the emotions have ways of thinking that are used by both animals and humans. Such as anger is useful for intimidating, dominating, and making others stay away. Cruelty is used to control others. Guilt is used to shame or belittle others. Fear is used for safety reasons. Sadness is used to evoke compassion and elicit favors. This is the mind of children under the age of 10. The intellect kicks in after 10, however, most will continue to use their emotional mind throughout life.

The emotional mind is able to think by daydreaming. It's possible to create a plan, or solve a problem by simply daydreaming. Unfortunately, the solutions are not well thought out.

Brooding is another form of emotional thinking. That's where answers are obtained by focusing on a feeling, such as being unjustly hurt. A good answer may sometimes appear, but it's usually a dumb solution, like kill the offender.

Charming and conniving are clever forms of emotional thinking. It's where lies are being used to deceive others, such as when faking an injury. What's interesting is how many criminals think that conniving makes them smarter than others. What they need to consider is why lots of connivers are living in prison. So lying is not very smart.

The emotional mind is a seeker's toughest battleground, because daydreams start with a feeling. Consciousness then floats off on the wings of a dream. The emotional mind is mostly a funster mind, however, its opposite is the painster mind. The painster thinks in terms of gloom, doom, terror, and disaster. Too much of that happening and feelings of suspicion, distrust, and persecution will follow. That's the definition of paranoia.

20. INTELLECTUAL MIND

The ability to create thoughts is unique to the human race. It's what makes us superior to animals. Or to be exact, the intellect is why we became an advanced species of hairless apes.

The intellect is like a computer that operates on light beams. The spotlight searches for a memory, and a vision of it appears. Light up some more memories, and desire is then able to connect the memories together to create speech, possibilities, and mental pictures.

The very first use of the intellect appears around the age of 2. That's when children begin creating words out of sounds. After that, they learn how to create strings of words (sentences) that can make sense to others. A child's ability to communicate keeps on improving, but their mind continues to be a fuzz ball of fun until the age of 10. That's when they're able to think deeper, and better decisions can be made. Before that, they could only create answers by using the memory and emotions.

The lower intellect is a verbal mind. Add some

imagination, and a higher form of the verbal intellect is created. It's where a person is able to see what to say before saying it. Another form of the verbal intellect is internal talking, which is internally talking your way through a problem. What to say, or how to say it, can also be established by talking to an imagined person. The lower intellect is often used for creating stories, and the internal talker creates the story lines.

The middle intellect is where logical possibilities are created. Logic is a creative process that puts things together like 2+2=4. It's called deductive reasoning. The middle intellect can also do inductive reasoning, which is a process of elimination. An example is when taking a multiple answer test, and the answer is unknown. We manage to figure that A is not the answer. Neither is B or C. Therefore, D has to be the answer, because it's the only one left. The middle intellect is able to add, subtract, multiply, divide, categorize, define, discriminate, invent, and put together lots of possibilities. Those talents are useful for creating art, music, writing, math, inventions, and lots more.

The visual intellect is a higher intellect. This is like a stepping stone to the intuitive Mind, because intuition is also visual. Start out by focusing attention on a small area between the brows (the 3rd eye). Then focus on a question. The steps needed to solve the question usually appear within seconds. Then the middle intellect can take it from there to calculate an answer.

The 3rd eye is used for planning, because it can see the steps needed to complete a project, or solve a problem. The visual intellect is also able to mentally rotate an object, so as to see the other sides.

Most seekers have a high visual intelligence, and learn better by seeing than by listening. They are usually good at playing chess, because chess requires visualizing lots of possibilities. The visual intellect is also used for reading faces, interpreting sign language, and reading body language. An interesting thing about life is that even animals have visual intelligence. They appear to be dumb, but animals are superior to us when reading faces and body language.

It seems as though memories occur in the brain, as evidenced by stroke victims that suddenly loose their ability to recall. But there are cases where the brain doesn't seem to play a part in recalling, such as near death experiences. Those that die, and then return, will often recall seeing what others in the room were doing during the time of death. Another fascinating thing about the memory is when people recall experiences of a past life. Psychic phenomena also needs to be considered, such as when a psychic touches a ring, and gets a picture of the person who wore the ring. So where did the past life, near death, and psychic memories come from? The answer is, we have 2 memory banks. One is in the brain, and the other is in the intuition. Tha'‘s where everything about us is on file in God's Mind.

The next thing to consider is intelligence, which is recognition. All of us have taken intelligence tests, and anyone scoring high has bragging rights. But how real are the results of intelligence tests? A person could drop 20 points, if he had a hangover, and only a couple hours of sleep. Someone else could gain 20 points by being in peak shape, and having a cup of coffee. Another problem is the intelligence tests have to be changed every 10 years, because society keeps on getting smarter. The average score rises by about 6 points every 10 years, so a new test is needed to keep the mental retardation level at 70.

What blows intelligence testing away was a guy named Albert Einstein. Albert was considered to be retarded during childhood, because he was such a slow thinker. He even flunked algebra. Now Einstein is considered to be one of the greatest geniuses that ever lived. Einstein was an insight genius. He was able to slow his brain way down by doing deep inner thinking. Then the intuition would help out by providing an insightful answer. How the psychologists could ever measure insightfulness is unknown, because the intuition exists beyond the World of atoms and neurons.

A regular genius is different, in that his neurons are wired in fairly straight lines. As a result, the memories flash quicker from one neuron to another. That makes for faster than average thinking.

A Zen Roshi came from Japan to conduct our seven day sesshin. He was a lovable guy, but the Roshi would play games with our heads. He gave us a puzzle during the second day of the sessin. I spent about 6 hours trying to solve it with the intellect, and then went to him with my best answer. His reply was "Oh, I'm sorry you suffered so much with that puzzle". I was stunned, and then saw his point. Creating possible answers is a lot of mental work. The intuition works so easy that grinding away with the intellect is absurd.

The wheels of mind spin fast in highly intelligent people, but the wheels don't spin for intuitive people. Their mind remains calm and clear. Everything outside is calmly known because it is obvious. Attention is centered in the light of god's mind. All the seeker has to do is ask a question, and god will answer. Unfortunately, humans love superiority and greatness. They play many types of games to prove that they are superior to others. The very dangerous game is spinning the wheels of their mind up to a very high speed to prove that are more intelligent than others. An old adage is that there's a fine line between genius and insanity. When the wheels and intellect speed up way too fast, and they break apart, then insanity happens

21. CONTEMPLATIVE MIND

Contemplation is not a mind, but a type of thinking that's halfway between the intellect and intuition. A question is first needed. Then focus on the 3rd eye, and begin thinking about it. The next step is to deeply ponder on the question. That moves consciousness inside the 3rd eye tunnel to a space that's halfway between the 3rd eye and intuition. The intellect slows way down, during deep contemplation, and then starts **looking** for an answer. When the outer mind becomes steady, or still, then disconnect from the question, and move a little to the rear. That's when the intuition is entered, and you become the detached observer.

An answer may suddenly appear, during deep contemplation. It could be a picture of the perfect solution, or a knowing of how to do something. The benevolent Father in Heaven watched your intellect hit a dead end, and then decided to answer the question. Many artists, scientists, business men, inventors, etc use deep contemplation for receiving insightful answers.

Contemplation was often used to write this book. It should be noted that I spent 50 years studying different religions, and reading hundreds of spiritual books. But I finally had to give up the outward search for answers, because there's only about 10 good books on higher spirituality, and each of those books has an information limit. So the end of book learning had been searched. The only thing left to do was to get answers from within. That meant meditating, so as to become the detached observer. Then I would focus on a question, or on something intriguing, and an **insight** would appear. After the meditation ended, then a paragraph was written on what was seen. That was followed by 2 hours of rewriting the paragraph until it became clear and concise.

What's interesting about receiving insights is that the master DK said, "adepts and masters get all of their answers from within". He also said, "adepts don't bother to use the intellect. Contemplation is as low as their thinking goes".

Three strands of light enter the soft spot on top of the skull. One strand anchors itself in the brain center, thus creating a ball of light within the brain. The ball of light is god's intuitive mind. An imagination layer surrounds the ball of god's light with most of imagination shining forth in the forehead area. The next layer is intellect.

Imagination puts memories together to produce thought and recall. Unfortunately, desire likes to have fun by putting together thoughts that it wants to create. Emotions also create worry, fear, and anger, plus dream happy stories or proud dreams. Too much fun, greatness, Glory, superiority, and happy dreams produce an imaginary person or character. Continue dreaming all day, every day, and insanity results. Psychotic drugs help to control a wild mind, but meditation also works. Focus on the peaceful feeling of an outgoing breath, and mental peacefulness is felt. The brain becomes still. Another practice is to combine mental peacefulness with questions, and a contemplative mood is created. This is known as contemplation. The mind is being held still, then waiting for an answer to appear from god's intuitive mind. The advantage of being in a contemplative mode is things can also get done. This is a spiritual form of multitasking, only in this case, the intellect is being held still while god is doing needed tasks. Another way is to hold the intellect still and let god's love inside the chest do the talking. This is known as wisdom (loving understanding).

22. INTUITIVE MIND

God's Mind shines forth from a tiny point of bright light in the center of the brain. The tiny bright light creates a ball of light called intuition. The intuitive Mind sees forever. It's silent. It knows, and it thinks by seeing the greater whole, or the big picture. Then it's obvious how all the little parts work. The intuition also creates a feeling of just plain knowing, because everything is clear and obvious. This phenomena is sometimes referred to as "He knows all, yet he knows nothing". The knowledge came from out of somewhere, but there are no facts to back it up. Therefore, he knows nothing.

Things become intuitively **known** when the outer mind is still. An analogy is like being in a boat on a lake. Feelings and thoughts are like the wind creating waves. When the wind dies down, then the water becomes placid. That's when the fish and bottom can be seen. And that's when you'll **know** what's down there.

The intuition has a unique way of thinking. The

process of receiving a flash of insight is something like fishing. Questions are used for bait. Then it's necessary to watch and wait for the question to catch an answer. Sometimes it takes a minute to receive an answer. Then at times, it takes an hour, or even days, for an answer to appear. But in all cases, the outer mind has to be made placid and still before knowledge can flow through from the Mind of God.

Ideas originate from the Mind of God, and ideas usually appear as a quick flash of light. It's something like a camera flash. Most of the ideas flash forth during a long and hard intellectual struggle. But sometimes, an idea will appear after giving up on a problem. Then at times, an idea will appear while walking down the street. Sometimes it's seen in a dream at night, and sometimes it comes as a hammer that knocks you on the head. We often take credit for the idea, due to the mental effort expended, but God gave the idea to someone that's worthy and capable of making it work.

The last mind to consider is no-mind. This is not a mind, but a mental space that's close to the intuition. Breath following meditations are able to relax the brain way down to where there are no more memories bubbling up. Then the soul has to do all the talking and moving. However, the soul is very detached, and doesn't do much. So no-mind works well for living in a cave, but not so well for living in a city. Contemplation works better in a city.

At the end of the Zen seven day sesshin we had a ceremony, where meditators would say a word to describe their self, or something important to them. My mind was still and completely relaxed. When my turn came I had to say that I had nothing. The Zen Roshi then wrote on a six by six card something in oriental words meaning no mind. It meant I was completely intuitive. God was leading, informing, and speaking for me. We are now living in the age of Aquarius, which is the age of light, electricity, and Soul. Many will become enlightened during this time. It is also an age of mind, for many still are evolving from being intellectual to feeling intuitive. The process is to first get rid of the emotional mind, and its four painful emotions. The verbal intellect has to be controlled. That's done by eliminating excess talk. Remain the listener who adds a word here and there as you clarify and communicate. Talking is fun so allow others to have lots of fun, and remain silent as much as possible. The last part of mind control is to stop imagining. Remain the observer and listener. Then god will say a word or two and occasionally it's an urge to do something, or say something. Then things become obvious to the mind, being clear of thought. Occasionally there will be a psychic premonition of what will be happening, or what a person is thinking. This intuitive knowing happens on occasion, but it is the right thing to know, and it happens at the right time.

23. PSYCHIC KNOWLEDGE

Psychic abilities appear in 2 ways. One is by living in the now. That's when everything is more obvious. Animals are on this level. A higher level happens when consciousness enters the eternal now. That's when God's memories are available, and some astounding performances happen. However, psychics need to know that they are responsible for the knowledge received. It has to be used for helping others.

Becoming psychic often starts by developing a sense of time. A person automatically knows the time without looking at a clock. Such as knowing that it's lunch time, quitting time, or time to wake up. Next to be developed is a sense of perfect timing. That's when a person knows what to do, and when to do it. An example would be to automatically go to the door and open it. Then see someone walking towards the house. There was no knowledge that someone was coming, but a sudden urge to open the door was felt.

A silent voice can sometimes be heard from

deep within. It's the Spirit talking. All that's usually heard are 2 or 3 words, but it's enough to know of a better way to do something, or know how to get out of a tight situation. The silent inner voice is different than the loud voices that schizophrenics hear in their ears, which is internal talking of their alter ego.

The most intriguing displays of psychic knowledge happen when Spirit contacts one of the senses. Such as, a psychic sense of touch may develop for those that practice breath following. Or knowledge of future events may happen for those that practice deep contemplation. There's also psychic hearing, like when hearing the thoughts of others. The senses of taste and smell can also produce psychic knowledge.

Some become a psychic channel for an ascended being, but many channelers are pseudo psychics. They are able to contact the soul and sound psychic, but nothing of value is forthcoming. Their sessions usually start with lots of greetings and salutations. Then they say everything in a generalized and loving manner. Some wise things are said, but in total, almost nothing of value was conveyed. This is a case of using the Heart's Love and wisdom to sound psychic.

Natural psychics are able to easily retrieve information from the Mind of God, but if the motive isn't pure, then the psychic gets hurt. Edger Cayce found out the hard way by feeling sick, after giving readings on buried treasures. The readings were done for the purpose of splitting the treasure with the finder, but no one ever returned with riches. He also got debilitating headaches, during World War 2, after doing readings on German troop movements. Cayce died during the war, and some claim that his death was due to not remaining neutral.

Some become psychic by going into a super sensitive trance. That is hard on the brain and nervous system, but the trance psychics seldom know that. Many will open a psychic business, and then become hyper sensitive, neurotic, or even insane. Their trances were performed to gain wealth, fame, or to wow others. That is stupid, so no information will be given on how to become psychic.

24. CONTEMPLATION PRACTICES

I stayed at a Zendo where we combined the mantra MU with deep contemplation. I was to say MUUUUU all the way to the end of the breath, and then think, what is MU? There is an answer, but it can't be solved by the intellect. It can only be solved by the intuition. I worked on that riddle for 2 weeks, and then concluded that the koan was impossible. How can there be any output from a computer when there is no input? Almost all questions have something to do with something, but MU has nothing to do with anything. The question is so unsolvable that the intellect will eventually freeze. Then the intuition flips out an answer.

Below is a list of questions for deep contemplation. Try asking yourself, what is:

1. Truth
2. Good
3. Reality

4. Life

5. Love

6. Detachment

7. Centeredness

Pick one and spend a week, or a month, or even longer on it. Finding the answer is nice, but learning how to deeply contemplate is better.

Here's another one to ponder on. Everyone is a God, so who is answering the questions? Is it your Soul, or Spirit, or God Himself?

Fatigue, sickness, sleepiness, and weather can greatly affect a meditation. Even the Sun and Moon signs can affect a meditation. So it's best to go along with the flow. Do a contemplation practice during the high times, when the body is full of energy, and do a breath following practice during the low energy times, or if deep peacefulness is the objective. It's best to do a practice that feels right, for right now, and don't limit yourself to only one kind of practice.

25. THOUGHT CONTROL

So who are you. You are the light of god. At the very center of your being, God's light creates the imagination, and the desire funster creates your playful ego. That's how it works. Now it's time to grow up. Master DK lightly mentioned the not self several times in his books. I lightly studied with the intellect, but uncovered nothing deep. Now I am deeply looking at each dream that is noticed and recognizing each character that is not me, or not I. This practice works really good in separating soul from body feelings. Next switch to your soul which is more easily felt on the upper spine in between the shoulder blades. Just take consciousness rearward, relax, and you're there. Saying what is not ego initially becomes clear. At some point the question becomes, who is driving the body? Is it desire? Or is it ego? Many will say the ego, and hotly defend that position. However that is not true. Desire drives everything. The ego is merely imagining all the wonderful things that desire wants to see about itself. The ego is merely a mechanism for desire to have lots of fun and pleasure. It desires everything. So stop thinking that you're somebody great, glorious, wealthy, and powerful. For you are merely nothing other than desires fool.

The ego becomes obvious at enlightenment. What is first noticed is the ball of light inside the chest. Then comes a realization that this is your true self, which has existed for millions of years, which means that you are a divine being. Next comes a realization that the guy up front that you have always called John or Andy or wherever is an imagined self which is your ego.

Scientists have identified one cubic inch of brain matter resting on the mouth's roof as the ego. That's only partially true. It's really the verbal intellect, which ego uses to express itself. The real ego exists somewhere in the imagination. The left cortex may be the place. The ego is an imagined self, or it may be more accurate to say that the ego is the imagined self. The words I, me, myself, my, and mine are words we use to describe ourself. What's really being described is some aspect of the ego self, which is the dreamer of almost everything said, thought, and done. The verbal intellect only describes what ego wants to say, or think or dream.

Desire controls the whole body and creates ego.

There are two types of ego, talking and visualizing. Talking ego is located between the cheekbones and above the roof of the mouth. Talking is fun, because ego is driven by desire's funster. That's why monasteries limit talking. They prefer to have their students learn to talk with wisdom. That is when god is talking to the student, so the monasteries are usually quiet. However students are also learning to talk from soul's peacefulness. The emotions have to remain perfectly still to soul talk.

Ego is also located on the forehead center. Ego uses the intellect and imagination to create pictures.

We have to pause here to define imagination, as follows. The light of god's intuitive mind shines very brightly in the head's center. The divine light radiates the brains fuzz ball of nerves, which creates memory. The visual cortexes shine light on the forehead's nerve cells, thus creating both the visual intellect and intelligence. And imagination is defined as recognition, and the visual intellect is an area full of visual memories. Divine light shining on those memory cells creates imagination. The ego has a cell center near the visual intellect where it creates the words I, me, myself, my, and mine. These are ego's self descriptive words, so be aware that any time you say I, me, myself, my, and mine, your only find your ego. That doesn't happen when centered in the soul. Another thing to consider is how verbal intellect leads to daydreams. The imagination creates a story and jumps on the chance to have some story fun. Needless to say the 12 year funster is the one who wanted to dream. Another variant of this verbal and visual ego combo is the internal talking. That's where verbal ego is having fun talking to an imagined person.

We have four areas of the body that people like to identify as being their self. Women often say that they are their emotions. Men often think they are their pride. Some men think they are desire and muscle. Some think they are the mind. So we will define emotions, desire, and pride as being selves. However there is a fourth driver of self. It is the imagination. Enlightenment is when you're outer self is seen as being imagined or an imagined self. There's not much of a stretch to conclude that ego has to be an imagined self, or an imagination driver, that creates daydreams where yourself is seen doing great, glorious, and wonderful things. One more conclusion is needed. There is the question of who creates the story lines that go with each dream. Sometimes a story starts up the daydream. The story has to be created in the verbal intellect, which is just above the mouth's roof. Therefore the verbal intellect has to be part ego, or an extension of the ego's imaginings. So we have to conclude that thought control is ego control. Apparently, the ego is a seeker's biggest problem, so what can be done to minimize, or eliminate ego? Depression is an ego killer. The mind can barely think during depression, and can't gallop off having lots of fun. This is an excellent time to make changes in the personality and become a new person. It's a time when seekers see their lifestyle as being a barren desert. There's no meaning or purpose in continuing down the same road. Some seekers even surrender everything they have, including body and mind, to god. Their whole life is now devoted to helping god. They know that their whole future will be spent in poverty, but the seeker doesn't care about his future anymore. The nice thing about poverty is humbleness, which is another ego killer. Defeat is the third ego killer. Lofty ambitions are destroyed when defeated. Shame is the fourth ego killer. Being put in jail makes a person rethink his lifestyle. Social mistakes create embarrassment and regret, which makes a person rethink their position in the social pecking order. So in reality, that is good.

One problem is mental creativity. Another problem is desire likes to keep attention pointed outward.

When a toddler finally understands that he needs to be better at remembering things, then he instinctively focuses forward. After that, his self image starts to form; but attention is still too outward to be playing with self images. Ten is when the brain is mature enough to start putting memories together, so as to create possibilities. After that, kids learn how to combine their emotions, pride, and self image, so as to create glorious daydreams. Some kids begin to have attention problems at this time, because daydreaming is very addictive. However, it usually isn't a problem until learning how to meditate. Then the mind control battle begins. The ego wants to have some more daydreaming fun, while the soul wants to have a clear mind.

The left hemisphere of the brain is called the logical left. This is the ego's side of the brain. The right hemisphere is often called the emotional right, but it's really the soul's side. It's a reality side that thinks by seeing the obvious. A better illustration would be that the playful child lives on the left side, while the responsible observer lives on the right side. So when your meditation is interrupted by a dream, then move awareness over to the right side, and simply observe until the mind clears. After that, move back to the center of the head, and continue meditating.

The imagination is your playground and best friend. It's also your snake pit and worst enemy. But there's nothing wrong with the imagination. It's only a brush that paints pictures. Desire is the problem, because desire is always searching for some more fun and good feelings. The best tools for controlling desire are relaxation, detachment, and self awareness. Then to reach Pure Mind, the ego has to be taken down to nothing.

The imagination is often a pleasurable toy that creates a cheap high. Nothing has to be purchased to feel lots of mental pleasure. There's also no waiting, for it takes only a second to start up another glorious movie. Everything is good during a daydream. It could be as bizarre as slaying your enemy, but from desire's point of view, that's good.

The desire self is a hard one to control, because desire whines and cries until it gets what it wants. However, some things can be done about it. Fasting works well for making desire behave, but desire returns after the pleasure of eating is resumed. Will power also works, but desire returns when will power weakens. A more permanent way is to develop awareness of any wishes, hopes, or cravings that cross the mind. Also, think only in terms of needs, instead of wants.

Desire has a tendency to move upward, and unite with the chest's emotions. Then the funster is created. The belly funster loves food, dancing, and ball games. The chest funster loves talking, music, alcohol, drugs, romance, and parties. The mental funster loves pride, greatness, glory, and self admiration. When the childishness of a funster is finally seen, then it disappears. That's because childishness looks stupid, and nobody likes to see their self as being stupid.

The hardest part of mind control is making pride disappear. Then most of the ego disappears. Pride is a hard one to defeat, because the feelings of superiority, greatness, and self admiration are very pleasing to the ego. The feeling of glory also needs to be studied, because the brain releases lots of pleasurable chemicals during a glorious daydream. Fortunately, pride will disappear, when seen, because it's childish fun.

God's Good has a huge effect on the psyche. The interaction of Goodness with the chest creates feelings of pride and superiority. The energy of pride also moves up to the brain, and creates feelings of greatness and glory. So it's necessary to start studying the feelings of greatness and superiority. Then the feelings will eventually be seen as they start to form, or erupt. That is the best time to swat down pride, because (A), a proud dream can be eliminated before it forms, and (B), interrupting pride, as it starts to blossom forth, will eventually result in the complete elimination of pride.

The answer is to become aware of what the emotions, desires, and ego are doing. Examine and categorize each dream mood. and trends will appear. Such as, most of the daydreams are worries. That's a psychological weakness which needs to be studied. When the problem is fully understood; then worrying will disappear. That's a big relief, but it's not the end of daydreaming. Lots of other pleasurable and painful moods have to be studied.

Examining thoughts create knowledge about the outer self, and each bit of knowledge is like a building brick. When the stack of bricks is high enough, then you're able to see over the walls of the intellect. That's when a flash of **insight** suddenly appears. The outer self was seen, and what needs to be changed is obvious. After that, you become a better person. So **insight** is the magic wand of psychology.

The words **I** and **my** are red flags. Sometimes the word **I** has to be used to describe something, but it's usually an indicator of being focused on the ego. Then at times, the word **my** may be heard in the thoughts and speech. That's an indicator of being focused on ownership of possessions, body, looks, feelings, and relations. The problem with ownership is that it's the most common delusion of society. The reality is, "You can only rent", or you can only be a caretaker of possessions. So awareness of the words **I** and **my** will help a lot in eliminating daily delusions.

The final task is controlling the attention spotlight. Fortunately, attention can be kept away from the ego by studying and observing. That's fairly easy to do during meditation, but it's a lot harder to do during the rest of the day. So one answer is to observe what you are doing, like observing the feeling of the feet touching the ground while walking. When shoveling, observe the shovel, and arms moving the shovel. When eating, watch the spoon digging into the soup, and moving it up to the mouth. Then observe the taste, and grinding of food. If there's nothing to do, then read a book, or study something on a computer. Watching TV also works, if it's an unemotional program like science, technology, or history. Attention can also be controlled by designing, planning, inventing, or troubleshooting. The bottom line is, don't allow your ego to **play** with the imagination. Be the observer as much as possible.

Being the soul means living in a calm, detached, and mentally still space. What also works well is a calm, detached, and mentally focused space. If intellectual thinking is needed, then the soul can engage the intellect, and calculate an answer. Otherwise, the spotlight is not being used. Neither are the desires and emotions. That is when the outer mind is totally controlled.

Self entertainment is why people dream, and the dreams are created in your ego center which is located above the roof of the mouth . That's where the verbal intellect loves to create stories all filled with pleasing desires, hopes, fun, and cravings or emotional stories of greatness, glory, pleasure, happiness, or pain. So study desire's love of greatness, superiority, ambition, and power. These feelings will slow down or disappear when realizing what you're creating. The emotional feelings of pride's greatness will also be less when realized. The same thing happens when studying emotional pains and pleasures. Then at some point, self entertainment, which is a story created by the verbal intellect, has to be studied. It's being done by the love of dreaming, and dislike of boredom. Keep on studying the love of stories and they will also diminish. Avoid fictional books and movies.

Desire moves the muscles. Desire also drives the mind to imagine all those wonderful feelings that pop up. Controlling daydreams seems to be an impossible task. Willpower doesn't work, for that is desire suppressing desire. So try self awareness. Realize that "I wanted those dreams. The dreams are my desires". The dreams will stop happening when taking responsibility for what you're doing. The trick is to keep desire away from the imagination, then there is no ego. Self awareness is also needed for that trick.

Try to remain centered in the soul all day, every day. Do it by switching attention away from the mouth and imagination, focusing on the spine, mostly upper spine for that is where the large nerves are at. Your soul is half light of spirit, and half nervous system, so that is where the soul energy can be more easily felt. The practice feels like kicking back and relaxing. Just pay bare attention to what's out there, and remain attentive to your soul feeling. When walking, driving, or around others then be a little more attentive. When having to speak then let god speak for you. That is known as wisdom. Switch attention back to the imagination only when having to reason or calculate math. Focus attention on the hands when writing, typing, or preparing meals, on the arms when having to lift, saw, pound, or dig. On the feet when having to walk. Get your exercise by working an hour a day. A lot can be accomplished in a year by working just an hour a day. Then spend the rest of the day meditating, contemplating and cruising.

Eating is another problem. Pay no attention, or very little attention to the tummy. Eat as little as possible in the morning and only when the stomach is wanting to eat. Then eat only a small meal, or snack that helps to keep desire low.

A spiritual center exists between the forehead and the brows. It's the third eye. Light from god's intuitive mind shines forth from that spot. There's another energy spot on the forehead, an inch or two above the third eye spot. Over in India, it is called the eye of Shiva, and is thought to be a spiritual spot. But alas, this spot is not spiritual. It's an imagined ego spot. The outer part of the spot is like a movie screen, and deeper inside the brain there is a movie projector. Daydreams are projected onto the screen about yourself and yourself is seen doing great and glorious things. So this could be called a self image spot, however it could also be called the ego spot, because ego is an imagined self. Recall that there are two egos, the verbal ego and the imagined ego, existing in different spots. The verbal ego resides in the roof of the mouth and the imagined ego in the spot on the forehead. For some it is a playground, and for others it is a realistic thinking spot. To complicate matters more, it is an area of the brain that psychologists have already named as home to the ego. This is different from the mouth ego that is located above the roof of the mouth. The ego is a good name for it, but I think it could also be called the verbal intellect.

In order to become spiritual, you have to stop using the imagination. That has to happen before enlightenment can take place. Then the light within your chest can be seen daily. What turns off the divine light within the chest, to never be seen again, is resuming daydreaming. Then a fall from grace happens. To be a little more exact, you have alcohol, sex, and marijuana, but never go back to playing with the imagination again. You can walk, run, talk, read, and write, but don't be having fun by daydreaming. An interesting thing about being centered in the soul is there's no boredom.

Unfortunately, I now have to give a sermon. I hate sermons and now I have to give one. The problem with humanity is almost everyone is on a quest for more fun and pleasure. Humanity is obsessed with entertainment. It's all due to the 12 year old child on the front side of their body. If they are not having fun, they become bored, and have to self entertain by daydreaming. Too much of that and they slip away from being a little crazy to becoming very crazy. The solution is for everyone to get serious, but only a few will ever respond. Sermons and criticism won't work, so I don't know the solution. So it's up to god to straighten up his kids. Even the ninety year olds have to straighten up. Daydreams steal consciousness away for a pleasant ride. When you finally realize that you're dreaming, then end the dream, and move up awareness back to the intuition. This will be a daily fight for control, but eventually you'll enter the intuition to stay forever.

Caution. Use the practice of moving rearward

toward intuition only for slowing down dreams. Because it can create depression. This is not to be used as a shortcut to being more intuitive. The best and safest way to higher spirituality is to calm the mind, and hold it steady by using the mantras HU and HUM. That also moves attention away from the imagination and rearward towards intuition. During the day, try to remain relaxed and peaceful. Depression is a bad case of black feelings, due to working too much or even by studying too much. A vacation is needed, or some kind of change that makes life more interesting. Getting drunk, or high, also works, because you're having fun again. Changing into something interesting or fun is the best way to get rid of the boredom or burned out form of depression. These forms of depression are similar to, yet not the same as loss of imagination. What can be noticed when deep in the imagination depression is that you have no future. There's no ambition, no desire to talk with others, and no desire to do anything. Everything is black and gray, and the rain keeps falling. The intellect can pull you out. Try designing something. Do a lot of the designing in your head. Then start putting it down on paper. That helps to get the imagination working again.

A big problem with daydreams is they are futuristic. That sounds like a petty argument but know that dreams are what we want and what your 12 year old boy wants, namely another form of fun. To get rid of your boyish fun, start seeing the futuristic trait in each dream. This practice helps to map into the inner consciousness. Say future every time it shows up in a dream and a lot of your imaginings will stop appearing. Self-realization is the best role for changing the way you think, so keep on looking for where your mind is at, and a lot of dreaming will be ending. However the side of losing your future can lead to mild depression. That may also be good, because it also makes people change their way of acting and thinking and relating.

Higher spirituality means thinking differently. It's a matter of slowing down the intellect, so as to be intuitive and internal. The internal talker has to be shut down or used sparingly. The happy 12 year old boy, who loves to yell, cheer, talk loudly, boast, and talk a lot, has to be controlled. It can be done by eating a lot less and fasting. Less energy is then available and the boy has to discard his superiority and personality. You can't be running with the big dogs anymore, so he has to be sitting on the porch.

Less food means less muscle, and also means less chest energy. That also helps to slow down talking. People that talk a lot have an excessive amount of energy in their chest. Not only do they talk excessively, but the extra energy also pops up their pride, which increases internal talking and more stories, which become daydreams. So less food means less desire, ambitions, superiority, greatness, and Glory dreams. Plus less talking and internal talking. The thinking slows down. It is easier to make the mind sit still so as to be more intuitive. Meditation also helps a lot in controlling the internal talker, especially when studying each dream that crosses the horizon. Increase self awareness by studying each dream. Dissect each dream down into categories, such as desire, ambition, wealth, power, superiority, greatness, Glory, utopia, building castles, anger, fear, etc. "Knowing thyself" is very important in controlling your mind. Set in your mind that you don't want to have any more of those kinds of dreams. Know that the spirit within you is your master of change. All you have to do is know what needs to be changed. Firmly set the mind to do it, and it will be done during deep sleep at night, and you'll be a new person when you awaken in the morning. Desire is the culprit that loves to daydream, so the battle with daydreams is a fight to control the pleasures of desire. Some people can get total control in almost one minute, while it may take months for others. It really comes down to a fight between desire's pleasures and the righteousness of your soul. Desire has lots of power, while soul has lots of internal energy. So don't allow desire to do your thinking.

Characters reside a lot in the front side and can be deleted by doing a deep study of them, when they are seen in the daydream. However, two cannot be eliminated by self awareness. Those are internal talking to imagined people and the imagination itself, for internal talking is itself a dream. It has to be eliminated by relaxing. Deeply relaxed and then turning focus rearward to the soul. That imagination is another self awareness to be eliminated. I spent two days focusing on the imagination, so as to find a way to delete it, but no way was found. The imagination can only be eliminated the old fashioned way by meditating. The attention spotlight has to stop focusing on imagination by turning rearward to focus on the soul. So when a dream interrupts, stop the dream and turn attention rearward.

However, willfully switching attention rearward

can be dangerous. Irritable feelings and headaches can result. It's best to first breath count up to seven, so as to get peaceful. Then shut out the frontside and sink rearward to the peaceful soul. Most people will conclude that their out of control mind is caused by the imagination, but that is not true. The imagination is innocent. It is like blaming the hand for stealing something. The problem is self image. It is so much fun that dreamers want to keep the daydream going. It's due to yourself being seen saying and doing great, or glorious things. So don't blame your out of control mind on desire, pride, or emotion.

The nice thing about death is the realization that the mind and body are not you, that beyond this reality, beyond your imagined self, you are soul.

26. TIPS FOR SEEKERS

This is a scattering of topics that could be of value to seekers.

The World religions teach a method for quickly getting spiritual. It's turning attention inward, and talking to God in prayer. Some seekers are not interested in praying, because God knows everything about them. So why talk to God? That's a good point, but the beauty of prayer is the quickness in which a person can go within, and become centered in their Heart. Praying also works well for those that enjoy the inner feeling of devotion.

God hears all prayers, and will give an answer. It may come as a deep knowing feeling, or as a psychic flash, or as a serendipity moment. It could also come through a friend that says or does something. Even no answer says something. It could be God's way of saying later.

Surrendering is another way to quickly become the soul. The practice is to contact the peaceful Heart, and say "thy Will be done". Consciousness then surrenders to divinity, and you become a minister that lovingly knows what to say and do.

Most people prefer to relate in an affectionate and happy manner, but detachment makes the soul look cold and aloof. The way around this gap is to contemplate on loving kindness, for kindness is a quality that both Love and affection have in common. Another practice is to contemplate on sympathetic joy; which is joining in with others during joyous occasions, like at a birthday party.

Spiritual experiences happen during meditation, and some of the experiences are so fantastic that you'll want to tell everyone about it. That's a mistake, because most will conclude that you are being a braggart. Worse yet is if someone becomes enthralled with your experiences. Their reverence, praise, and devotion can get to be sickening. So it's best to keep all spiritual experiences secret.

Souls seldom look in a mirror. As a result, some seekers look like homeless people that live under bridges. Appearance means a lot to society, so occasionally check the appearance. Also, remain invisible by looking like an ordinary person. That means no robes, turbans, long hair, or bowing to others. The only thing that can't be hidden is the soul's peacefulness.

Muscle movement is a destroyer of mindfulness, because attention has to focus on a muscle. Contact with Mind is then lost. The solution is to move slower, so as to remain peaceful. Then the inner self has to do the work. Eating is another problem. Try watching the breath while eating, for that stops the mind from wandering off to another land. Talking also destroys mindfulness, because (A) attention has to be focused on what's being said. And (B) flashbacks of what was said can create a daydream. The solution is to talk very little. A sentence, or a few words, is usually all that's needed.

Lots of jobs exist that involve working on puzzles. Such as technicians, engineers, and scientists have to deeply ponder on perplexing problems. That puts their head in a good place to remain deeply thoughtful, and intuitive. But to go deeper, it's necessary to start living the spiritual life. That's where the road splits. It may mean having to leave the job, house, and wife behind, so as to be on the spiritual path. Jesus recommended "giving everything to the poor, and following Him". That works well for followers of a guru, because they then know where to go, and what to do.

So where does a seeker go when he's on the spiritual path? The answer is to find a spiritual group. But if there's something wrong with the group, or guru, then pack up and go on to another one. Life is for learning, so living in different places works well.

Christian ministers have long known that devotees passing on to higher levels would often experience depression. There's a story in the bible of a wealthy farmer who lost his crop of grain, his cattle, house, and family. The reason was that god did it so Job could be free to become highly spiritual. The spiritual depression problem happens when a seeker is getting close to changing from human to soul. Humans think with their intellect, which is driven by desire. Souls have a different way of thinking. They think with the intuition, however, they are able to use the intellect when needed to calculate a math problem or plan something. Afterwards, they prefer to move back to the intuitive mind and let god do the thinking. Another difference is souls, masters, and on up are serving the will of god. That's a nice job in that all they have to do is help others. Spiritual depression isn't always caused by a disaster. It could also be due to guilt, shame, or even being fired. In either case a person has to rethink his lifestyle, and hopefully choose a more spiritual lifestyle like getting more involved in church activities, or joining a commune. Some even surrender their life to god, and allow their self to be led by god. They will then know what to do and where to go. All they have to do is ask god for directions and god will help. It's that simple.

We are masters of our own personality. We become what we want to be, and discard what we don't want to be. Once a conclusion is made, the change usually takes place during sleep at night. Sometimes it will happen right now, and sometimes it will take a week like with tobacco and drug addiction. The problem for seekers is they have to discard their happy and fun fun fun personality of childhood, so as to become the peaceful soul. Not only the fun filled child has to be discarded, but their highly involved intellect also has to be discarded in favor of the knowing mind of intuition. However, the intellect can still be restarted when needed. The futuristic mind of being human also has to change in favor of the soul's here and now thinking, or attitude. Giving up your happiness and mind is tough, but giving up your future so as to be a servant of god is where a lot of depression is felt. Eventually the seeker will see the stupidity of struggling to being a superior and outstanding person. Than his feet will start walking the path to higher spirituality.

Depression is caused by guilt, shame, loss of wealth, loss of a loved one, rejection, and other ways. The skies become dark and there is no future. However depression is very valuable, for it makes a person want to change his ways. They start going to church. Some even surrender to god by wanting god to do all the talking, thinking, and moving the muscles. Their ego and personality have totally collapsed, and they are firmly on the spiritual path. What now interests them is helping others. The changes in a person's life happen in two ways. One is a deep, dark depression, and the other is self-realization. Going to a psychologist or doing it your self via self study can create flashes of insight where yourself is seen and the "answer" is obvious.

27. RIGHT LIVELIHOOD

Enlightenment is when seekers are living in both the human and soul Worlds, so a different way of relating has to be created. One of the soul problems is that deep peacefulness makes it harder to talk. Another problem is that deep detachment makes a seeker look cold and aloof. Also, too much profound thinking can make a seeker look like a "cold fish". And in addition, paying only bare attention to the outer World doesn't always work well. So a soul personality has to be created. Learning how to be a little outward in this or that situation is the answer. A smile, a greeting, or being interested in others works well, because others then have something that they can relate with. An added benefit of creating a soul personality is that your Spirit will be using it, after becoming an adept.

It's hard to remain totally centered all the time, because we need to provide the body with food, clothes, and shelter. Staying in a cave, and living off the land, is not an option. I tried that, and found that I had to compete with animals for any edible food.

They got most of it, and winter was coming. That meant there would be almost nothing left to eat until spring arrives, so I had to discard the caveman lifestyle. However, it should be noted that the meditations were very good during those 10 days.

How can anything get done when a person is remaining peaceful, detached, and mentally still? Actually, a lot can be accomplished by doing very little. Such as, intuitively seeing the whole of something can save a lot of time and effort. Then there's wisdom. A few words of wisdom can easily convince others of a better way to do something. It can also save hours of talking. Another nice thing about wisdom is that it can perceive worthless endeavors, like competing in sports. All a person receives from winning is the feeling of triumph and superiority. Those are childish rewards, so doing nothing can sometimes be better than doing something.

Living in a competitive world is tough, because the detached soul can't keep up with speedy people. Employers want workers that move fast, and get lots accomplished, but moving fast destroys centeredness. Fortunately, the soul has wisdom, peacefulness, patience, and helpfulness. A lot of jobs exist where those qualities are in demand, like working in a customer service department. The advantage of being there is that you don't have to work hard and fast. Just be pleasant and helpful.

Most of the jobs are in business, and the soul has some tools that businesses want, such as deep thinking, insightfulness, and intuition. Employers love to have workers that provide good ideas. Then in the higher positions of business and government, the quality of wisdom is vitally needed. So a soul infused person will sometimes rank higher than speed, experience, and youthful energy.

The ideal situation is to spend your life helping others. I found that being a caregiver is a good profession, because the qualities of Love, joy, patience, harmlessness, and humbleness are needed. Being a caregiver was my solution, but I am not you. So some thought needs to be given as to what works best for you. Spend some meditation time contemplating the 7 paths, which are:

1. Science
2. Religion
3. Healing
4. Teaching
5. Arts

6. Finance -The lending of money for projects that will benefit the community, nation, and mankind.

7. Politics (governing)

You are **not** limited to being only a guru after enlightenment happens. Neither is an enlightened person destined to become an outstanding leader. Soul infused people are needed in all walks of life. So don't limit yourself to just one way of helping mankind.

The problem of starving is remote for seekers, due to being so close to God. Knowledge of what to say and do will be there when needed. Buddha owned only his cloak, sandals, and a begging bowl. He never worked, plus he advocated a lifestyle of homelessness and begging. Jesus is another one that didn't work. He also owned only his cloak and sandals. It's possible to live that way today, but those guys lived in a different Age. Back then, spiritual beggars were acceptable. Now it's a different story. We are living in a stimulating Age that's full of wonderful machines. A huge storehouse of knowledge is on the internet, so studying and being creative, will be the norm in the Aquarian Age. The Piscean Age tendencies of Love, devotion, and peacefulness are still important, but being talented and mental is now a higher priority.

Having a good job is important, but seekers need to take some time off for peace, solitude, and contemplation. A two month sabbatical every other year works well. I found that camping on the shore of a beautiful lake is the place to be, and watching the water is a wonderful way to remain the detached observer. A lounge chair that tilts back works best, because land around a lake always slopes downward. Take along some spiritual books to ponder on, because there'll be lots of time to deeply contemplate.

It's best to camp on the shore of a lake that's more than 200 yards (meters) across. It's because the distant shoreline looks like a flat line, and looking at a flat line steadies the mind. The horizon line of an Ocean, or a prairie, also works well for quickly steadying the mind.

Bears are the scariest animals, when camping. Skunks can also ruin a camping trip. Unfortunately, most of the wildlife problems are created by campers leaving food on the table at night. That's easy pickings, and the animals will be returning every night, in hopes of finding another tasty snack.

Bears can become obnoxious and dangerous.

Some ranger districts take responsibility for their animals by rounding up the dogs, and hunting down any bear that raids a campsite. But most of the ranger districts do nothing to protect campers. Knowledge about which districts are responsible, and which ones are irresponsible, is not published. So it's best to protect yourself by carrying a pepper sprayer at all times. Pepper sprayers have been proven to work better than guns against bears, however, the best solution is to put all food in the car trunk every night. Then there's seldom any problem with hungry animals.

Flies and mosquitoes are the biggest problem. Bug repellent works well, if you can stand the smell. Flyswatters also work, but squashing a pesky fly isn't always necessary. Just whack 'em away with a flyswatter. The fly won't come back if it was a close call.

Campground noise can be another problem. Especially when a group of party animals camp next to you. The solution is to take along a pair of earplugs.

Long meditations were the highest points of my life. The next highest points were the months spent in solitude beside a beautiful lake. Returning to work after a sabbatical was always enjoyable, because it felt good to become a worker bee again in the giant beehive of society.

28. HEALING

We all face the problem of what to do about the ever weakening body. Allergies are limiting us to a smaller variety of foods. The joints begin to hurt. The mind can't recall certain words, and the body doesn't recuperate like it used to. It's been a slow downhill slide ever since the age of 30. After 50, it's a much faster downhill slide. And after 70, there's only a small amount of vitality left.

We think of illness as being something bad, but sickness makes people want to change their ways. As a result, many seekers get started on the path, and stay on the path, to become healed. They intuitively know that higher spirituality is the best way to heal their illness, but that can take years. So in the meantime, it's best to have a doctor diagnose the illness. You may buy his prescription drugs, or do it the safer way with herbs and nutrients. Either way may work.

Many MDs limit themselves by concluding that disease is caused by bacteria, genes, and heredity. Other healers also limit themselves, such as, Chiropractors say that sickness is due to spinal misalignments. Naturopaths claim that disease is due to toxins, nutritional deficiencies, and a low immune system. Psychologists perceive illness as being caused by stress and emotional problems. Acupuncturists claim that sickness is due to excesses and deficiencies of energy in the meridians. There's some truth to all of these theories, but in reality, a lot of sickness is caused by exhausting your energy on wants, emotions, and pleasure. It has been proven that many illnesses are caused by **excess** beer, cigarettes, drugs, work, and food. Also, many illnesses are caused by **deficiencies** of sleep, exercise, cleanliness, warmth, companionship, and good food. Everyone knows that is true, and everyone knows what their excesses are, but many ignore the obvious. They go to a doctor, and the doctor then has to inform them that smoking, drinking, or whatever, is causing their problem.

Doctors can't heal you. The body heals itself. Doctors only **assist** in the healing process. So it's best to go to a library, or to a health food store, and read books on nutritional healing. A missing nutrient may be the problem. The do-it-yourself attitude works best, because it's **your** body, and **you are** ultimately responsible for the health of the body.

MD's need to be the first ones visited, because they have the technology needed to figure out the name of a disease. If the illness is close to killing you, then stick with the MD. If the illness is moderate, then go to a library, and look up the disease. Sometimes an herb or nutrient will work, and sometimes it won't. If not, then start doctor hopping. An acupuncturist, naturopath, chiropractor, or psychologist may have the answer. If all else fails, then the MD's medicines and surgery will have to be the answer.

Prescription drugs give fast, fast, fast relief. That's what everyone wants, so drugs appear to be the best answer. But what most don't know is that drugs seldom cure an illness. That's because almost all drugs, herbs, and nutrients are allopathic. The word allopathic means that the substance makes you feel better, but it has to be taken daily, so as to be relieved of sickness. So the first choice should be with nutrients and herbs. If those don't work, then take the prescription medicines. Those are toxic, and that's why drugs are locked up at drug stores.

The word cure is tightly controlled by the FDA. To them, a cure means forever. We all know that vitamin C cures scurvy, and vitamin D cures rickets, but the FDA doesn't allow that to be said. That's because it's possible to become deficient again in vitamin C or D. We have to live with that definition, because the FDA will jail anyone that claims to have a miracle cure.

Significant is another word to understand. Significant is often used in reference to a study done on a drug, herb, or nutrient. We commonly think that significant means a big improvement, but in reality, it means about a 15% change. Researchers usually test for both a drug effect, and a placebo effect. They may find that 30% on a drug claim to feel better, and 10% on a placebo claim to feel better. That's a 20% difference, so the drug is described as a significant improvement. But what's not being said is that 70% felt nothing. The time to get your hopes up is when something is said to be "greatly improving". That's about a 50% improvement. But it also means that 50% felt nothing. So the only thing to do is try it. If nothing happens, then try something else.

Lets not overlook psychology, for it's possible to destroy your health with excess emotions. An example is the liver and gall bladder are harmed by anger. When the anger problem is fully understood, then anger disappears. A couple weeks later, the pain also disappears. That means psychologists are healers. Or to be more exact, the client healed himself, and a psychologist helped.

Everyone is still alive and aware after death happens. They have no pain, and are in perfect health again. That means death is also a healer. So what's the logic of a person working hard all their life, and then spending all of their money on a surgical procedure that prolongs their miserable life for a few more years? People fear death, but that doesn't have to happen. We die every night when falling asleep, and nobody fears that. The fear of death is mostly caused by selfishness. The more attached a person is to their possessions and pleasures, the more they fear death. So the answer lies in learning how to detach.

Some suicides are wrong. Anyone doing it to escape from depression, or guilt, will experience the soul's disappointment. That's because each lifetime is a golden opportunity to become like the soul, who is always hoping that you'll make the change. On the other hand, suicide is honorable for someone that's too feeble to take care of their own needs. School is finished for him, so there's no use hanging around the school grounds anymore.

You'll eventually feel the soul's energy, and know that you have the ability to heal others. Soul healing is done by sending your Heart energy to the ailing area on a patient's body. Another way is to send your Heart energy to a chakra on the spine that serves the ailing area. Both ways work, but be aware that it's dangerous to send energy to an inflamed area, because inflammation indicates excess energy. So it's best to first feel for excessive heat. If the area is hot, then use cold water, or ice, to heal it. Another dangerous practice is to send soul energy to a cancerous lump, because the lump will only grow larger.

I tried soul healing on some friends. One was a woman that had lung problems. I sent my Heart energy down the arms and to her lung area. Afterwards, she felt great. But later that day, she had an argument with her lover. She insulted and screamed at the poor guy for 6 hours. Then she came back saying that her lungs felt bad again. She wanted another healing.

Another example was a friend that had stomach problems. I did a healing on his stomach in the same way. Afterwards, he felt fine. Later that evening, he went to a drinking and dancing party, which lasted till dawn. About 10 hours later, he was back asking for another healing. That's when I stopped doing spiritual healing. I feel compassion for the suffering of others, but it's best to let the common folks work out health problems in their own way.

The disadvantage of becoming more spiritual is that the chakra energies change when consciousness changes. That can cause illness. The common man doesn't have any problem with chakra changes, because his consciousness remains fixed at a 13 year old level. But a split happens when a person becomes aware of their Heart. Many of the probationers will attend church to fan the glorious feeling of divine Love into a greater brilliance. That makes the Heart feel real good, however extra energy is now flowing from the belly up to the Heart. The lower belly energy may cause indigestion, constipation, headaches, and intestinal pains. So it's best to start eating a better diet. Also eat a smaller amount at each meal, because the weakened intestines can easily plug. If that happens, then the next day you'll be feeling tired, foggy, and grumpy. If the tummy doesn't want to grind away on food, then wait until noon to eat. Or if the innards feel really bad, then fast until they feel good again.

Seekers need to be cautious about excessively focusing on the 3rd eye, because doing it can cause eye problems, headaches, sinus problems, and mania. When a seeker becomes accustomed to extra 3rd eye energy, then those problems will go away. However, it's best to take it easy. Don't overdo any meditation practice to the point where excessive stimulation occurs. If that happens, then switch to the peaceful breath following practice, or even quit for a while. Higher spirituality takes years to attain, so don't harm your self by pushing too hard.

There are 4 ways to equalize energies. One way is to make an appointment with an acupuncturist. Another way is to recharge the brain and nervous system by getting lots of sleep. The third way is to remain relaxed all day. A nice thing about remaining relaxed is it makes you more a beautiful and likable person. The fourth way is to meditate. That rejuvenates the body in a different way than sleep. It feels like recharging the batteries. The key is to make the breath ultra slow. So slow that only a slight feeling of the breath touching the nostrils is noticed. That's when the soul is entered, and then everything equalizes.

29. DIET

A vegetarian diet is an absolute must for becoming enlightened. Eating meat is a form of cannibalism; in that, animals are like our little children. Animals want to survive, and their intelligence is in the range of a 2 or 3 year old child. But the best argument is known at enlightenment. That's when Life within everything is seen, and then it's obvious why we shouldn't destroy the Hearts of our younger brothers. That includes birds, fish, worms, and insects. In short, nothing that breathes oxygen. On the other hand, there are times when eating meat is ok, such as when lost in a forest. It's better that you survive than a slow moving snake. Eggs and dairy products are ok, but it's best to go easy on those products.

Plants breathe carbon dioxide, so that puts them in a different category. Plants don't like being harmed, but we have to eat something. Besides, a plant's role is sacrifice and service to the higher beings. Fortunately, there are lots of foods available that don't involve harming plants. Such as trees give freely of their fruits and nuts. Shrubs give freely of their berries. Grain crops die, and are then harvested. Root crops die, and are then dug up. So lots of foods are available that don't involve harming plants.

It should be known that vegetarians can become deficient in vitamin B12, creatine, and carnosine. Those nutrients come mostly from meat, but that's nothing to worry about. Those nutrients are also available at health foods stores.

Studies have shown that calorie restriction will extend life span by 40%, if started at the age of 21. The lifespan can also be extended by 20%, if started during middle age. And no matter what the age, health greatly improves within 2 weeks after starting a low calorie diet. Going without food activates certain genes and anti-stress proteins. Then the organs slow down, and get some rest.

What works well is to eat until two thirds full. **Never** eat until stuffed, because the innards are being grossly stressed. That's an important point, because the belly is the body's dynamo. It has to be kept in good shape, and the best way to do it is by limiting calorie intake to less than 1,000 a day. More if you have to do lots of hard work, or if you live in a cold climate.

Good digestion is important, because lots of partially digested food slips past the intestinal walls at each meal. Then the immune system has to clean up the mess. Too much of that happening, and the body begins to feel sluggish, or sick. So eat only small meals.

Keeping the body supplied with all of the needed nutrients is important for anyone over 60. However, the most important things are hormones, for those little things are basic to good health. Seniors face the problem of their hormone production decreasing down to 10 or 20% by the age of 70. So a regular check up is needed to keep the hormones at a safe level. The more dangerous hormones are obtained by prescription only, but there are ways to get around some of the prescription hormones. Such as, selenium, iodine, and L-tyrosine are foods for the thyroid. That's important to know, because low energy, coldness, depression, dry skin, and other ailments are caused by a low level of thyroid hormones.

The pituitary gland is a bigger problem, because the production of growth hormones decreases by 50% every 7 years. That means you're getting almost nothing by the age of 70. That's bad, because a lack of growth hormones is why an old body shrinks. Even the internal organs and brain shrinks during old age. Fortunately for seniors, the pituitary gland is capable of manufacturing enough growth hormones to fill the body's needs. Unfortunately, the organ gets lazy, during old age, and doesn't want to squirt out enough to do the job. So the answer is to buy a growth hormone stimulant at a health food store. Or consume L-Arginine, L-Ornithine, L-Lysine, and L-Citruline before bedtime. Those are foods for the pituitary gland.

A word of caution needs to be inserted. **Don't overdo any of the hormones, or stimulants,** because excessive amounts can also create an illness. The safest way is to see an Endocrine Doctor about adjusting your hormone levels.

Each of your cells contain tiny mitochondria. Some cells have 2, while others have as many as 5,000. Mitochondria are important, because they are the body's power generators. They take in carbohydrates, and convert it to electrons. However, the ash left over, from burning carbohydrates, lacks an electron, and will rob one from a molecule, cell, or DNA. The ash is called oxidants. If an oxidant robs an electron from a DNA, then the cell becomes cancerous. If an oxidant robs an electron from a low density cholesterol lipid, then it becomes sticky, and can stick to the wall of an artery. Too much of that happening, and the arteries become plugged. The solution is to eat a wide variety of fruits, veggies, nuts and grains to get the many different types of antioxidants.

Different colored fruits and berries contain different types of antioxidants which are healing to different parts of the body. Fruits contain the highest amount of antioxidants, and the darker the color, the more they contain. Another solution is to buy some antioxidants at a health food store.

It's best to eat raw foods, because cooking destroys its nutrients. If a food has to be cooked, then microwaving works best, because the cooking time is a lot less. Steaming is next best, and that's followed by boiling. Frying and barbecuing should be avoided, because that creates lots of oxidants and carcinogens.

Avoid meat, because that's the dirtiest food. Meat contains the dead animal's oxidants, plus, cooking adds more oxidants.

Everyone needs to study natural healing, because many illnesses are caused by a deficiency of nutrients. Everyone should also know that it's now possible to substitute a safe nutrient for a prescription drug. So go to a library, and read about your problem. Then experiment to find what works best. Sometimes a nutrient works best, and sometimes a prescription pill works best. It's also possible for half of a prescription pill, plus a nutrient, to work better. If that's the case, then tell the doctor. He's a good person, and will be interested in hearing about a less toxic way to treat an illness.

Medical doctors have long known that cholesterol is bad. Yet cholesterol is made in the liver, and is used in a lot of body functions, so it is also good. Their next discovery is there are five kinds of cholesterol ranging from large to tiny. The tiny ones are produced by eating meat, and is the culprit in clogging arteries. That's bad, but hold on, for medical scientists are now saying that burnt cholesterol is the problem, so cooking very little seems to be the answer.

30. FINALLY

Living in a meditation center works best, because you're then living alongside other spiritually minded people. However, the teachers usually don't say much. That's where this book will be a big help. The first reading of any book gives a general knowledge. The second reading yields lots of specific information. So read the book again. A lot of effort went into making the subjects clear and concise, but sometimes, only the mountain tops were hit. Try reading after meditating, because consciousness is then more intuitive.

I see shortcomings in myself. The Dali Lama also admitted that he has shortcomings. Even Jesus didn't do well at times, like when he was furiously kicking over the money changers tables. Or the extreme worrying he was going through, while in the Garden of Gethsemane. Of course, anyone would get emotional if he was about to be crucified.

Spiritual Psychology will someday be taught at Universities. The soul is hard to prove, but lots of evidence is coming in from those having a near death experience. That proves we continue to exist after the body dies. In fact, I had 4 friends tell about dying, and then arising from their body. That means there has to be many more resurrected people out there. Someone researched the subject, and concluded that about 25,000 near death experiences happen every year. The high number is due to Medical Science becoming proficient at prolonging life. So by studying near death experiences, and by studying reincarnation testimonials, scientists will someday prove the existence of the soul. Then Spiritual Psychology 101 will be taught in Universities around the World.